Celebrated author and artist

A. Kendra Greene's *No Less Strange or Wonderful* is a brilliant and generous meditation—on the complex wonder of being alive, on how to pay attention to even the tiniest (sometimes strangest) details that glitter with insight, whimsy, and deep humanity, if only we'd really look.

In twenty-six sparkling essays, illuminated through both text and image, Greene is trying to make sense—of anything, really—but especially the things that matter most in life: love, connection, death, grief, the universe, meaning, nothingness, and everythingness. Through a series of encounters with strangers, children, and animals, the wild merges with the domestic; the everyday meets the sublime. Each essay returns readers to our smallest moments and our largest ones in a book that makes us realize—through its exuberant language, its playful curation, and its delightful associative leapfrogging—that they are, in fact, one in the same.

"*No Less Strange or Wonderful* doesn't so much live up to its title as explode out of it. What the amazing A. Kendra Greene makes of the world, what she makes *with* the world, is unfailingly wondrous and revelatory, whether her subject is the Santa Barbara Zoo giraffe, balloon-twisting royalty, the dog that became a speck, Ebenezer Scrooge, or the manifold metaphor of Senator Ted Cruz as a sentient bag of wasps. Prepare yourself to be dazzled by this most original of writers."

—BEN FOUNTAIN,
author of *Devil Makes Three*

"I'd follow A. Kendra Greene's writing anywhere—that's how confident, how surprising, how crafty it is. She is truly one of the most delightful essayists in the game, which is reconfirmed within the first few pages of this bold new collection. What a joy to never know where an essayist of this caliber might take you next: to the zoo, to a balloon-twisting convention, to a tony Dallas Christmas party with its own bespoke Scrooge. You also might get taken to ontological places, emotional spaces, and other spots impossible to pinpoint on a map. Carry this fine book in your handbag, your knapsack, your marsupial pouch, and crack it open when you want to be transported."

—ELENA PASSARELLO,
author of *Animals Strike Curious Poses*

"I am so taken with A. Kendra Greene's takenness with things—funny-looking dogs, delighted devils, monotremes, the toes of the Universe, beautiful frozen toilet water. Her intoxicating book does the opposite of diminishing the world, and it took me to new places. Like a train that spurns conventional stations, conventional tracks, this book plunges into the wild, trackless unknown."

—AMY LEACH,
author of *The Salt of the Universe:*
Praise, Songs, and Improvisations

"A. Kendra Greene's newest essay collection is equal parts joy and surprise. The devil visits a bookstore. A dress made from balloons withers instead of pops. There are badgers with human hands, smells in the attic named Mortimer, a purloined bird specimen whose thief writes to say it's doing just fine. And we read along, caught up as much in Greene's language as we are in her knack for finding wisdom in the world's smallest mysteries, its hidden delights."

—SARAH VIREN,
author of *To Name the Bigger Lie:*
A Memoir in Two Stories

NO LESS
STRANGE OR
WONDERFUL

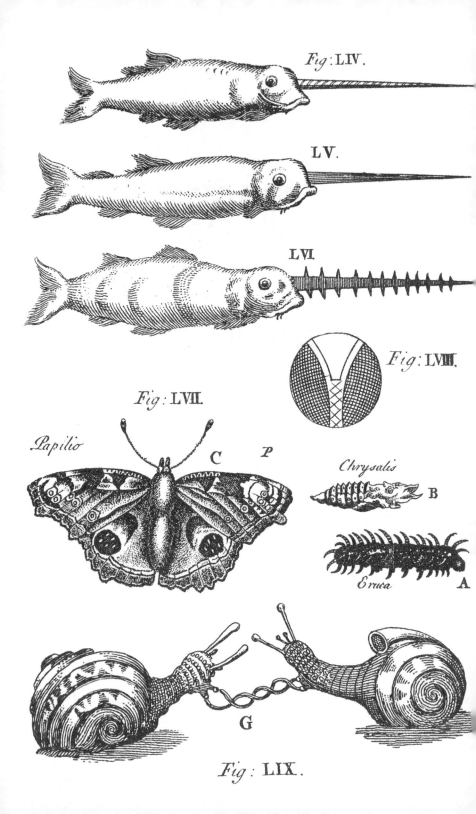

Fig: LIV.

LV.

LVI

Fig: LVIII.

Fig: LVII.

Papilio

C   P

Chrysalis

B

Eruca   A

G

Fig: LIX.

NO LESS STRANGE OR WONDERFUL

essays in curiosity

WRITTEN AND ILLUMINATED BY

A. KENDRA GREENE

TIN HOUSE / PORTLAND, OREGON

Copyright © 2025 by A. Kendra Greene

First US Edition 2025
Printed in the United States of America

Cover image credit: Zoological Society of London. *Proceedings of the
Zoological Society of London*. Vol. 1. London: Academic Press, [etc.],
1904, https://www.biodiversitylibrary.org/page/31887274.

Manufacturing by Versa Press
Interior design by Beth Steidle

Library of Congress Cataloging-in-Publication Data is available.

Tin House
2617 NW Thurman Street, Portland, OR 97210
www.tinhouse.com

DISTRIBUTED BY W. W. NORTON & COMPANY

1 2 3 4 5 6 7 8 9 0

For all the luminous, far-flung,
astonishing loves of my life,
especially Ellen, who sees me—
Each voice who called out from the dark
when I was broken open

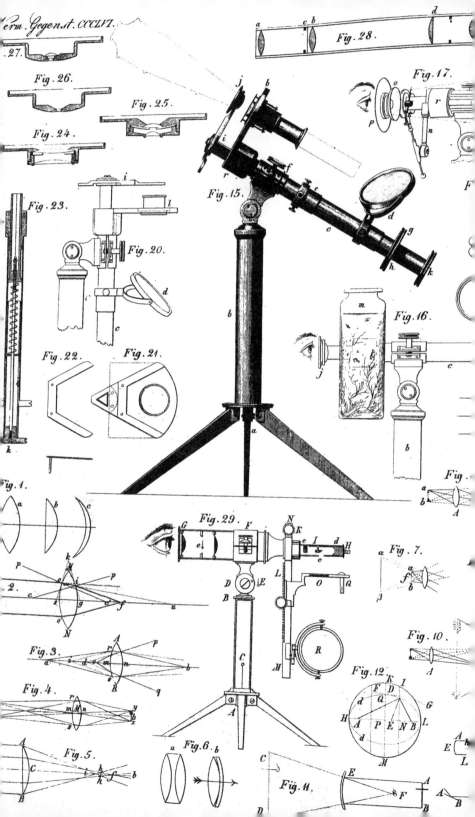

The soul will at least perceive physically things which
it has difficulty grasping mentally . . . what they
have difficulty comprehending with their ears,
they will perceive with their eyes.

—THE ABERDEEN BESTIARY

. . . as if it had shoved everything
aside to come into existence.

—VIRGINIA WOOLF

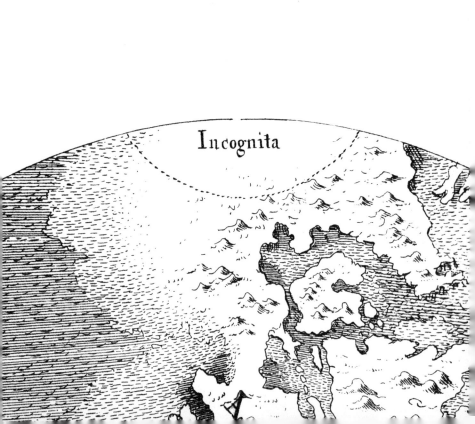

MANIFEST

NO LESS STRANGE OR WONDERFUL

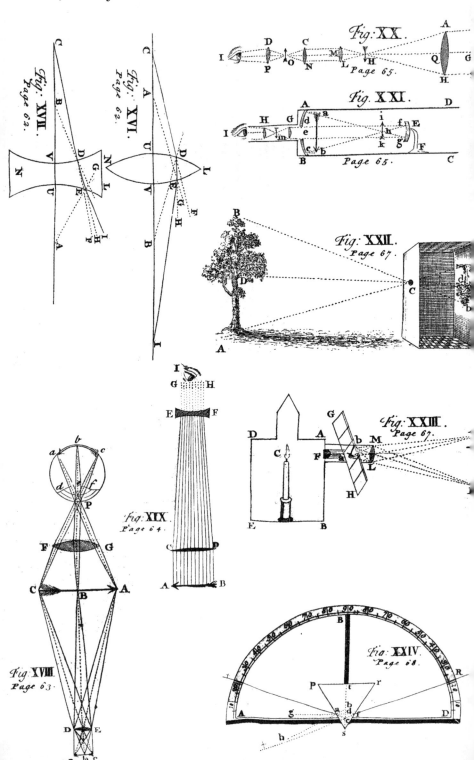

Plate. III.

Fig: **XX**.
Page 65.

Fig: **XXI**.
Page 65.

Fig: **XXII**.
Page 67.

Fig: **XXIII**.
Page 67.

Fig: **XVII**.
Page 62.

Fig: **XVI**.
Page 62.

Fig: **XIX**
Page 64.

Fig: **XVIII**
Page 63.

Fig: **XXIV**.
Page 68.

THE WITCHING HOUR

ONE NIGHT, THE FIRST SUMMER OF THE PANDEMIC, I WAS walking this very block. It was equally late, the same witching hour, when I saw a tree coming down the street. It was a young tree, slender and tall, not loping or thudding as you might imagine a tree to lumber, but gliding, just sailing along—dare I say, a bit jaunty? It seemed so carefree: the night to itself, a little wind in its leaves.

I was, in those months, generally unmoored from time. From so many things. I did not exactly think of myself as restless, or searching, but certainly I walked a lot, going out again and again, later and later. My book of hours was kept that season by the alarm of grackles at sunset, swarming an already darkening sky; by the tide of pickup trucks idling in the corner-store parking lot, its gravel studded and clinking with bottle caps becoming rust; by the basketball players shoulder to shoulder lining the court in the park, the border of their bodies, the way they glowed, skin shining under lights; by the utter stillness outside the hospital; by the chrysalis forms of figures come to sleep on the high side steps of the block-wide church.

At some point that night the vantage changed, a gap in the wall of cars parked between us, a revelation as the tree drew near. The tree was on a bicycle. The tree was riding in the front basket, like a friend perched on the handlebars, out for a lark. It moved so lightly. I have never seen anything so easy and sure.

I remember how little it changed for me, upon seeing more, the mechanics of the situation made plain. The whole thing was no less strange or wonderful for the dark rider I could never quite make out, propelling it all along.

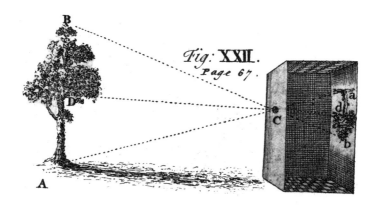

For with names the world was called
Out of the empty air.

—EDWIN MUIR

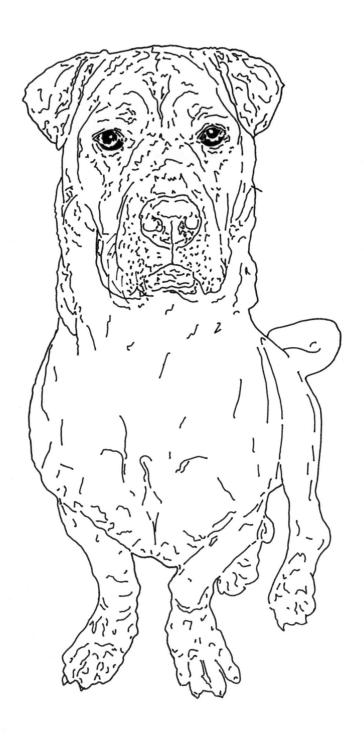

1

SPEAKING OF BASHEIS

CHLOE WAS A DOG BUILT LIKE A COFFEE TABLE. SHE WAS LONG
and broad with diminutive little legs. Imagine a magnificent
dog, the head and body as if rendered by one artist, the limbs by
another. Imagine a claw-foot tub. Imagine a dog as if on cinder
blocks, her proper legs stolen. Louise first saw her on the other
side of a little rise of grass in someone's backyard. Louise called
to the dog and assumed the creature would stand up and run
over, and the dog did come—but had already been standing.

This was shortly after my sister had fallen in love with Louise, and when they got the apartment together in Venice Beach,
they were close enough to my brother that he'd sometimes
come over and walk the dog. It was a perfect place to walk a
dog. A few blocks and you were on the beach, the beach with
that long sidewalk path, past the sunbathers and the bodybuild-
ers and the volleyball players, all the way to the Santa Monica
Pier, if you were in a mood to stretch your legs.

It was perfect, except for the fact there were so many people around, which wasn't exactly the issue, but somehow being surrounded by strangers seemed to give people permission to voice what they were thinking out loud, as if anonymously, thoughts totally uncensored. And they felt the need to say, with shocking regularity, "That's a funny-looking dog."

It was a strange kind of witnessing, these grown people moved to exclamation. It was almost like a reflex, an involuntary response, a "gesundheit" for funny-looking dogs. They made no eye contact, no effort to engage, yet these strangers somehow caught in both startle and trance were compelled to blurt out this eureka of the collective unconscious: "That's a funny-looking dog!"

We were discussing Chloe at dinner one night, Louise and my siblings and I, speculating on Chloe's origins, essentially in agreement that her ancestry was surely some variation of basset hound and shar-pei. We speculated further that she might be the peak specimen of her ilk, the bashei, and with the wine list handy christened her in absentia with a fancy breeder's name to make it official.

Cypress Merlot still had the same short, stiff, honey-colored coat as when she was Chloe. She still had a hard-whip tail that curled in a perfect half circle of contentment. She still had a floppy tongue and a thick skull. But now when a stranger in the grip of stream of consciousness announced, "You've got a funny-looking dog," my brother would graciously volunteer: "She's a bashei."

It changed everything to have a name. The posture of the stranger would improve. The tone of their voice would lift and soften. They might bring one hand to their chest in a modest gesture of surprise. "Oh," the stranger would say. "I've never seen a bashei."

My brother would then magnanimously offer the stranger an excuse, a fig leaf to cover their ignorance: "They're better known on the Continent."

It was very easy to talk about the bashei. I went for walks with my brother and the dog whenever I could. "That's a funny—" a stranger would start to say and we would interrupt before they could finish the thought with our new impregnable line of offense, "She's a bashei!" And suddenly everyone wanted to know about basheis.

"They are from France," we would say, with an unpracticed nonchalance.

"You know the dog in *Peter Pan*?" we would ask. "Well in the movie they made her a Saint Bernard, but she's based on a bashei."

"The bashei is really a product of the Industrial Revolution," we would expound, the words already in our mouths, the lecture arising impromptu and unbidden, fully formed, as if it had always been there. "With an increase in wealth and an emerging middle class, households wanted to hire servants; you know, emulate the social status of the well-to-do. But when they could not afford nannies for their children, they might still afford a bashei. They are bred to be the constant companion of children. You see her long, low back? You see how sturdy she is? The perfect assist for a toddler learning to walk."

The strangers loved us. They loved our bashei. They asked if they could pet her. They scratched her ears and cupped her head in their hands and told her how beautiful she was.

We would have gone on that way, forever perhaps, all windfall and astonishment, surely we would have, except for the woman who asked, "What kind of dog is that?"

"A bashei!" we said. It was almost a thing we sang by then, a gift we gave, a celebration of all that was right and good and possible in the world.

"A bashei!" we said, and the woman produced a boy as if out of thin air.

"Oh good," she said. "My son is very interested in dogs. He wants to be a veterinarian. He's never seen a bashei."

We had not known our limits, had no compunction about our ruse, until we realized that we could not lie to a child. We did not then stop to review, did not in that moment consider how invariably the people who pointed, who stared, who offered unvarnished observation so frank as to be rude, were never children. We had not until then considered ourselves as peddling untruths. Every bit of our embroidery had felt more honest, more right, than the steady stream of small slights against our dog. We quickened our pace and mumbled our regrets and did not look behind us as we rushed by. We stopped telling anyone anything about the dog.

But my sister and Louise still had the apartment in Venice. They still had to walk their dog. And sometimes, if they walked towards the ocean, a stranger would stop them.

"Is that a bashei?" the stranger would ask.

If the stranger had doubted before, here was independent confirmation. Surely it was a trend. Surely the bashei was the next golden retriever and soon we would all have them and everyone would know. My sister and Louise had no response. The stranger would double down.

"There's a redheaded guy around here," the stranger would say, "has one just like it!" The stranger would say it as if providing evidence, as if proving initiation—as if the two people walking their dog might be the ones unconvinced—as if they might be shown exactly what they had in that glorious moment, right there at the end of their leash.

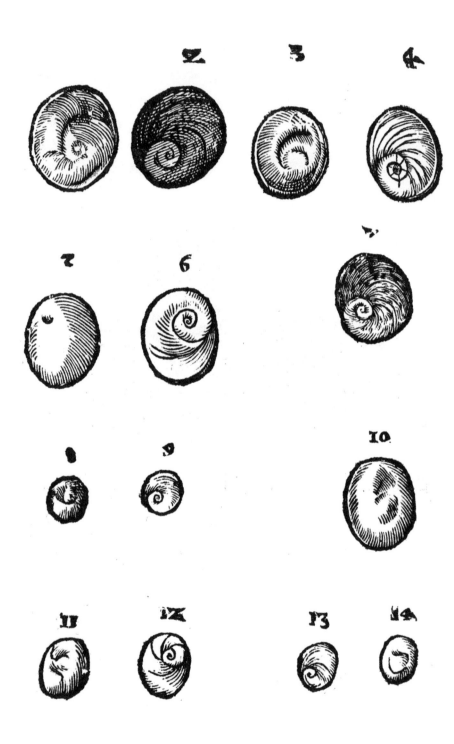

WINSTON BECAME A SPECK

10.

BACK WHEN WE ALL LIVED IN IOWA, YEARS BEFORE YOU WERE
born, your parents had a dog. It was the very same fluffy white
dog you have always known in your living room, the one who
lets you bury your hands in his coat and squeeze. Your dog,
even then, in his first living room, knew not to sit on the sofa,
that it was not allowed, but would sort of lean against it with
one haunch, then two, kind of back into it by degrees until, as
if he knew he had found a loophole, wearing the grin one only
has while getting away with something, the whole rear half of
the dog was entirely up on the sofa cushions and the front feet
had never moved from the ground.

Your dog, back then when we all lived in Iowa, was very
good friends with Winston. I'm not sure you know Winston.
Winston does not come to visit when Kerry and Will and Felix
come to visit. When they come to visit here, Winston goes to a

farm where a few of his brothers and even more of his extended family live in what I've always assumed is a very beautiful barn. Winston is a smart and sleek, rusty-colored dog.

After we all lived in Iowa, Kerry and Will lived in Texas, and so did I, and we thought it would be a great idea if we got together at the ocean at the edge of Texas, and that's exactly what we did one winter when it was not the least bit cold.

The rest of us had been many times to many different shores of many different oceans, but Winston had lived all of his life in Iowa and then Texas and had never, not once, seen the ocean. The ocean as I've known it in Texas gets brown as horchata, warm as bathwater, and so shallow you can walk out remarkably far before it's even up to your waist. The sandy shore that meets it is terribly broad and smooth and sometimes trucks drive on it and sometimes cars get stuck with one wheel spinning helpless in the air and sometimes there are long reefs of Christmas trees making sure the sand doesn't all blow away. I am more used to ocean beaches that quickly meet with rocks or cliffs or banyan roots, but this spreads out forever. It is expansive and vast and some days you look out and there is nothing to interrupt it.

I don't know if it was the look of it or the smell of it or the sound of it, but the first time Winston set paw at the ocean, Winston was amazed. Winston seemed not to know what to do with himself. Winston did not know if he should snap at the salt in the air or the salt in the water, did not know whether to step in the sand or the waves. It was too much and too strange and it was entirely overwhelming.

And then, like that, there was no more indecision. Winston saw a bird.

Winston took off after the bird, paws drumming down the sand at water's edge, and just before Winston could reach the bird, just a second to spare, the bird lifted up into the air and gently flew away. We could see the disappointment, the surprise—but just a flash of it. Winston slowed almost to a stop, watching it go, but just as he might have come to rest, out of the corner of his eye he glimpsed another bird, a little farther down, and Winston bolted in pursuit.

And just before Winston reached this new bird, it, too, lifted up into the air and gently flew away. Winston slowed again, almost to a stop, watching it depart. Some things are always out of reach. So many things drift away. But then once more, out of the corner of his eye, he glimpsed *another* bird, and Winston took off after *that* one.

Every time, he almost got there, and every time, the bird flew away, and every time, Winston nearly stopped, but every time, just as he might have come to rest, he spied another bird and was off.

There was always another bird. Each sighting carried him to the next. Winston ran and ran, bird by bird, farther and farther down the endless expanse of sand, getting smaller and smaller until Winston became a speck.

We could barely spot him. We could hardly make him out. We worried the cycle was unceasing, and we worried we would never see Winston again. I'm not sure we could see him at all when we inhaled all at once, then shouted all together, as loud as we possibly could: "WINSTON! COME HOME!"

The sky and the sand and the sea were hard to tell apart at that distance, all of it a kind of sun-blown haze, and we didn't know for a while if anything had happened. But then, slowly, we could see it. We could see Winston the speck start to get bigger, become a dot and then a dog, his legs flying in a blur as he ran and ran and ran all the way into our waiting arms and we held him in the biggest hug.

9.

ON OUR WAY HOME FROM THE ZOO, THE PACIFIC ROLLED BY on the passenger side, obscured now and then by stands of eucalyptus and knots of windswept cypress, occasionally an off-ramp. My thirtysomething-year-old friends were in the front seats. My four-year-old friend and I sat in the back, one of us in a car seat, and having exhausted all conversation about having fed lettuce leaves to the wiggling lips of craning giraffes, the great pillows of dung we'd seen fall out of the elephant's butt, and the very important fact that, however it may appear to the untrained eye, gibbons *are not* monkeys, I was casting about for more to discuss.

There may have been other stories I told that afternoon in the car, or maybe this one struck a nerve and eclipsed all other topics. The part beyond doubt is that after I told it, my four-year-old friend wanted to hear again and again that day, again and again in the days that followed, would sometimes weeks later arrange a video call exclusively to hear, "when Winston became a speck."

It was sweet the way my young friend said *speck*, with that care and reverence one has for a new, perfect word. I assumed she asked for the time Winston became a speck in part because it was fun to say *speck*, the way she could draw out the sibilance but couldn't help but pop-crack the end.

I told this story so many times that I came to amuse myself in varying it. I leaned into the repetition or the imagery, focused on the characters she knew or the one she didn't, added extravagant tangents or embellished every detail, made it stretch until dinner or made an exercise of stripping it down to its essence to see how very short a story it could be.

My friend, on the other hand, was unvarying. She always requested, in the same words, "when Winston became a speck." She never exactly corrected me, never quite said that one version was more satisfying than another, but I told it to her so many times in so many ways I began to see it was the speck she craved. It was, in fact, the speck that mattered.

8.

MY FOUR-YEAR-OLD FRIEND WAS THE TYPE OF PERSON TO take great interest in butterflies visiting the garden. The whole family had galactic roles to play in her astronaut-inspired Halloween costume. In the weeks before she was born I sewed an orange dinosaur, and when she was past gumming its felt appendages she would later retrieve it from the toy basket and give it a little purple hat before inviting it to tea. When I showed her the sea glass I had found in the sand, she announced each nub a mermaid's gem. Now she all but squatted down to get closer to this story and squint.

She would have already known the itsy-bitsy spider, and all three little pigs pitted against one big, bad wolf. Surely, on innumerable occasions, she had previously declared herself a little teapot, and she would have noticed what grows and what shrinks. Maybe no one understands smallness better than a child. Maybe no one is more invested in scale. Certainly my friend was old enough to grapple with what is and what isn't. We start early on the vital project of what is fleeting and what will stay.

7.

WE HAVEN'T ALWAYS KNOWN HOW TO THINK OR SPEAK OR write the idea of naught. Note the other nine numerals of the Indo-Arabic system are older, written 9 to 1 and nothing else. But where we've felt a need for null, we've tried over and over to give it shape. And we've found so many forms it might take.

The Babylonians used a blank space or three hooks or borrowed from punctuation two wedges at a slant. The Mesoamerican glyphs include a partial quatrefoil and what is sometimes described as an empty turtle shell. Chinese counting rods used an empty space, and the knotted-cord accounting of the Inca knew the absence of a knot. The initial N was used in Roman numerals, sparingly, perhaps only in an eighth-century table drawn up by the Venerable Bede.

The ancient Greeks sometimes used a lowercase omicron in their astronomical work, temporarily, before the final calculation was recorded, but largely they avoided a symbol or a numeral or a placeholder of any kind, seemed unable to get there before they satisfied the existential paradox: How can not being be? Nothingness first got a numeral in ancient India, where Alex Bellos suggests it is no coincidence that the concept of nirvana had long since taken hold. The mystic symbol has since met all kinds of resistance. Even typewriters at first made no distinction between the elliptic numeral *o* and the circular letter O, didn't waste a key on that.

6.

IN MY TWENTIES I HAD A CONTEMPORARY NAMED RAINBOW. Her parents had been of the conviction that a person ought to name themselves, stalled off giving her anything official until she had enough language to claim it for herself. It strikes me as exactly the sort of name someone early in their experience of the world would gravitate to, that native impulse to align with something bigger, however passing.

As a grown-up person, she stood by it. She liked Rainbow. It was a good name. She was asked about it all the time, of course, but remained patient, unburdened in the telling. It was no trouble to explain it. She knew who she was.

My four-year-old friend, in a different position, made a different calculation. Or I suppose she completed the arc. I don't know about her deliberations, but my four-year-old friend knew that names matter. She was resolute in defining herself. When she announced, on her terms, what we should call her, she picked the smallest thing that counts.

5.

ENGLISH HAS HAD THE WORD ZERO SINCE 1598. IT STARTED as a noun, the arithmetic symbol sometimes voiced as "oh." Two hundred years later it gained the power of an adjective, and a century after that added its status as a verb. What began as absence, the point of departure in reckoning, then expanded, if only slightly, until it also contained an act of concentration.

We get an early glimpse of zero in Pingala's ancient treatise on Sanskrit poetry, all those light and heavy syllables, moved in every combination, imagining longer and longer words. His *Threads of Knowledge* hints, too, at those golden ratios we now associate with Fibonacci, and this spiraling to or away from is one of the ways we approach nothingness.

It is the work not just of poets and mathematicians, but of philosophers and scientists and skywatchers and timekeepers and adventurers making maps. As a point of reference, zero tares the scales. In decibels, we've set it at the threshold of hearing, below which we are unable to detect. In temperature it can be the absolute floor of possibility or just the border of frozen solid and fluid melt. In the sounding data of nautical charts, the average tide defines zero, a zero made out of myriad tides, a thing not marked on charts by any number, only inferred where the shading of water meets the shading of dry land. This story might be like that: a point of reference, a thread of meaning, an inflection point. It feels like a tether as she climbs into the diving bell to study the abyss.

4.

IF I HAD SAID "UNTIL WINSTON BECAME HARD TO SEE," OR "until Winston was really far away," or "until Winston *appeared* no bigger than a speck"— if I'd been interrupted before the line where Winston was restored to us—if by accident or felicity I had made any other little shift in the language, she might never have asked for the story again. But here it was. Resting on one tiny little word. And any other story I might tell void.

It dawned on me, telling after telling, that she was studying the map of this story, weighing its evidence. She seemed to be gathering data. She was, I think, not so much imagining the visual effect of distance on the human eye; she was testing a vanishing point. She was peering out at the imperceptible. She was considering the stone-cold fact of a creature traveled to the brink.

3.

IT BEARS SCRUTINY, THIS BUT MAYBE ALL THINGS WE SOME-times seem not to notice or accept or believe. Certainly, diminishment surrounds us. Origin too. Disappearance is a matter of both longing and fear. I mean, isn't this the root of magic: what can vanish—and what can be made to appear?

2.

THE ANCIENT EGYPTIAN SYMBOL *NFR* REPRESENTS IN ITS depiction the heart and trachea. It means "beautiful" or "pleasant" or "good." In measurement it is the baseline, the point from which all else is measured. It is the center of the tomb. It is the center of the universe. It is ground floor and starting point. It is our first written form of the concept nil, comes before its numeral is ever a dot or a circle or anything else. It is a beginning from which the rest radiates out. I love that it is rendered by the body, by those vital centers of beat and breath. It suggests to me the moment before speech itself, makes me think of that cylinder space the trachea holds open, and the heart as a place of chambers ever emptying.

1.

"WHEN WINSTON BECAME A SPECK," MY FOUR-YEAR-OLD friend asks of me. Over and over. Insistent. Insatiable. Exact. Over and over, until it becomes a kind of constant.

"Again, Zero?" I ask her.

Zero repeats, "Again."

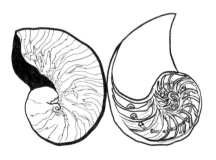

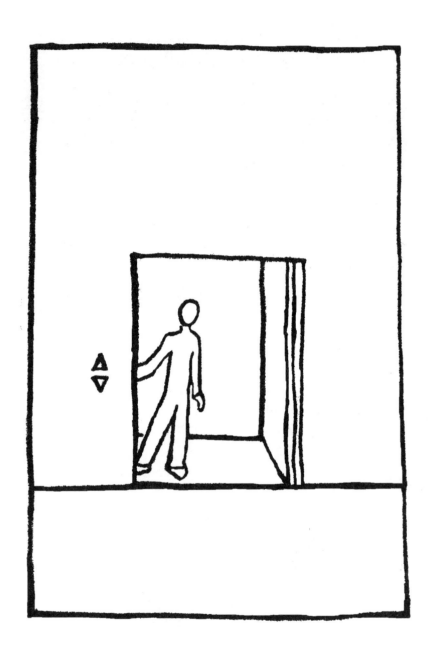

LOVE IS IN THE AIRPORT

I WASN'T LOOKING FOR LOVE. CERTAINLY NOT IN THE PARK-ing garage between the last stop on the CTA Orange Line and check-in for Midway's departing flights. It didn't matter. I didn't have to. Love found me.

Let's dispense with the misconceptions: Love does not stink. Nor is Love blind. Love won't actually lift you up where you belong—though he will offer to carry your bags and he'll make sure you find your way to an elevator.

Love, it turns out, is tall and lanky and quick to smile. He wears a uniform. Love introduces himself and asks why your boyfriend isn't there to shoulder the heavy bags for you, if maybe you're at this very moment on your way to see such a man? Then, when he's hefting your luggage—Love insists—Love tells you women today are so strong they don't even need men. The weight Love takes from you is significant, but Love doesn't complain. In fact, he seems impressed.

I almost wished in that first blush, in that moment when Love was new, that I had someone to leave for this stranger. I could hear the breakup in my head as I tried to explain to an imaginary sweetheart, "I thought I loved you, but really, I'm only in love with Love!"

But as we walked into the terminal, I already knew I would follow Love no farther than that. Maybe I knew that this Love, stooped under the burden of all the books I had packed, wasn't strong enough to last.

Or maybe it's that he came on too strong? I wasn't in the habit of giving out my phone number, or of being asked for it, and when he did, Love surprised me, made me nervous. My stomach fluttered and I started to stammer. I looked at the floor.

It must be death you can't bargain with. Love was willing to make a deal.

"Okay," Love said, and he seemed both patient and kind. "You don't have to give me your number now. But if you see me when you come back," he began to prophesize, "if you come back on that return flight and you see me and I see you—" He locked his gaze on mine and paused for effect. "Then it's a sign. A sign I was meant to have your number." He didn't blink. It was less a question than a statement of impending fate when he finally proposed the bargain. "And then you'll give it to me?"

Who was I to argue? Only a fool quarrels with Love.

"A sign," I agreed. It seemed fair. It seemed true. "It will be a sign."

And as suddenly as Love had come into my life, I was then set free.

He leaned the oversized red duffel to the linoleum floor and, how simply things happen, walked away. A ticketing agent waved me down the counter so I could present identification and collect my boarding pass and it was then, no better reason than a bag to check, that I turned my back on Love.

The distance between us bloomed another two thousand miles. I moved over mountains. I reached an ocean. My thoughts stayed with him. Say what you will about the Love of a lifetime. About the power of Love, especially young Love. Go on about his labors and his gifts. Tell me, as if I didn't know, about Love lost.

WILD CHILEAN BABY PEARS

I USED TO PLAY A GAME AT THE END OF PRINT VIEWINGS where I asked the visiting class what they would take home from the museum. I varied the scenario. Maybe it was a reward for having been such a great group. Maybe everything suddenly needed to be saved from a fire. Or maybe, for reasons of my own, I was just going to look the other way. What I kept constant was the constraint: "Just one thing," I would say. "Don't be greedy," I would add. And then twenty or thirty individuals would sweep their gaze across the mats and frames of twenty or thirty photographs I had spent an hour pulling from the vault.

It did not matter who wanted the series of New Mexico lowriders in the red velvet portfolio box or who wanted the big, grainy black-and-white print of a tree on a bank shot from underwater. What caught my attention was the young man who asked which one was the most expensive. Or the kid who determined which would be the easiest to carry away. I liked these answers, these moments when someone remembered out loud that the images were objects, that however they moved in the life of the mind, they were also, always, things in the world. And things, so very many things, can be taken home.

The point of asking was that there is a difference between things you visit and things you live with. What you love in a museum you could hate at home. What is striking in a tasting can fall short as a meal. Some of the best movies I have ever seen, I never want to sit through again. But of course, it can also go the other way; some things, some precious few things, will nourish and feed you forever.

IN THE 1970S, WHEN THE FEDERAL RESERVE WAS ISSUING Bicentennial quarters and railroads were painting train cars red, white, and blue and everyone with a match was shooting off fireworks, the University of Iowa Museum of Natural History chose to honor the Bicentennial with an exhibition of American species endangered and extinct. This was the same cultural moment in which the Smithsonian opened the National Air and Space Museum, the United Kingdom loaned Congress one of the four known copies of the Magna Carta, and the Musée du Louvre lent an exhibition of 149 liberty-related works to tour the Detroit Institute of Arts and the Metropolitan Museum of Art in New York.

That the Iowans thought of loss when they thought about their country strikes me as strangely touching. What could be more patriotic than an informed critique, a call to activism and reform? What is more American than innovation and consumption and their twin wakes of unintended tragedy? What does the patriot do but grieve? Whatever their motives, what is clear is that they chose to exhibit extinction, focusing on historical factors, and as they endeavored in this manner to talk about loss, they filled a room full of stuff.

Stuff, in this instance, meant exhibition cases and wall text and so on, but most importantly it meant mounts: the taxidermic specimens of so very many species going, going, gone. Gone, except they weren't. Not entirely, not if you count their skins.

EXACTLY ONE SPECIES IS KNOWN TO HAVE GONE EXTINCT IN the whole history of Iceland, a span of one thousand years. That species is the great auk, and we know exactly the day it happened. We know the names of the two men who strangled the breeding pair on July 3, 1844, and we know the name of the third man who crushed their solitary egg with the heel of his boot. We know the end of the great auk line because the very scarcity of them spurred on a frenzy of collecting. Collectors, eager to complete their collections before supply ran out, pushed prices up and up. And so birds that had been hunted for food were hunted as specimens. And if the specimen of a rare creature is valuable, the specimen of an extinct one is priceless.

We say *extinct* when the last living member of a species dies, but their properly preserved skins will last for centuries, never mind their bones. These species don't live on, by any means, and yet a tangible part of them remains with us. More than a sesquicentennial since their extinction, we still have great auks, at least to the degree that we still know the whereabouts of seventy-eight skins, seventy-five eggs, and twenty-four complete skeletons still in existence around the world. We don't know where the skins of those last two great auks ended up, but we know the address in Copenhagen to visit their internal

organs and their eyes. What we don't have is a word for after extinction, for when we lose whatever's left.

THE IVORY-BILLED WOODPECKER WAS GENERALLY BELIEVED to be extinct back in 1924 when, glory of glories, a Cornell ornithologist and his wife found a nesting pair in Florida. Then, even before the scientists decamped, two local taxidermists took out a permit and quite legally shot both birds.

The ivory-billed woodpecker was listed as endangered in 1967, even though the only suggestion it was still in existence at all was an East Texas field recording of what might have been its call, or might have been something else. Indeed, a confirmed sighting of the ivory-billed hadn't been made in decades when the University of Iowa chose to include it in their Bicentennial exhibition. It was simple enough to curate: the museum staff looked over the three ivory-billed specimens in the collection, picked the best one for exhibition—good size, feathers in good shape—and left the other two skins in their gray cardboard storage box.

A skin, in this context, is just what it suggests: the skin of the bird, plus all the feathers in the skin and usually the bony bits like the legs and beak, and part or all of the skull. All the wet parts, the organs and the tissue and the fat, have been removed and replaced with enough cotton to restore the skin to its approximate volume in life. Until you look too closely, the bird seems whole. Limp, maybe, drowsy even, but whole. As if the body could still startle awake at any moment. And the skin can be stored like that for ages, with the right dimensions but the wrong viscera, cotton tufting from the sockets where eyes should be.

Only when fit over an armature, given glass eyes and sewn up, does the skin become a mount, and it is the mount that one sees on public display. It was the mount, not even the bird, that in 1979 entranced one Iowa visitor in particular. The mount sang like a siren—until the visitor could no longer keep his hands to himself.

THERE IS HARDLY A MUSEUM I VISIT WHERE I DON'T WANT TO touch things. Never in a museum where I've worked, as it happens, but forever where all things textured and dimensional are put on display. Shells and ceramics and chrome. And not just touch. There are things in the world so glorious, so appealing, so bright or smooth or splendid, I want to put them in my mouth.

THE IVORY-BILLED WOODPECKER IS ALSO CALLED THE LORD God bird, or the Good God bird. Unlike the whippoorwill, named from its own song, this bird is nicknamed for the utterance it inspires in the person who sees it, the sound it draws from another mouth. True, they are big, but not so much bigger than the more common pileated woodpecker. With only a few skins and a few black-and-white pictures to work from, I cannot tell what made them so exclamation-worthy. Yet still I begin to wonder if it is their rarity, or their divinity, that makes them known also as the Holy Grail bird.

THE VISITOR HAS NO NAME. NO DESCRIPTION. SO I WILL CALL this visitor: Visitor X. I assume Visitor X was already familiar with the Iowa museum. I assume Visitor X had seen this very display more than once, had come back again and again. I assume he did not mean to take the ivory-billed, not at first. No,

I assume there was no premeditation, that Visitor X did not case the joint, that Visitor X had made no special note of the lack of cameras, the lack of guards. I assume Visitor X was alone.

In pictures the ivory-billed is directly over a bleached bovine skull, halfway up the right end of a shared case. Why this specimen and not the passenger pigeon or the heath hen or the Eskimo curlew? Why not the pair of Carolina parakeets at the far end of the case; why not the shotgun and the shells and the powder horn alongside them?

I assume the ivory-billed was glorious, was lit just so. And I assume Visitor X was overwhelmed, was intoxicated with awe and longing and grief. I imagine there was a moment, just a moment, a flash as Visitor X realized this idol was an object and, feeling only devotion, without thinking anything else, reached out.

He would have used two hands to take it. He would have put the first hand on the prow of the bird, cradling its jutting chest, and he would have cupped the other hand around its base, lifting it up and out of the case. There would have been no violence in its capture, every movement quiet and clean, the bird tucked gently under one arm and walked out of the museum as if nothing could be more natural. As if this happened every day.

It was reported on a Thursday morning. It would have required twisting out three Phillips-type screws from the display case and moving the glass.

A COLLECTOR I KNOW HAS A PAINTING I ADORE. AS THE COLlector explained it to me, the painter had a beach house in the family. The painter sent Pantone books to half a dozen family members and asked each of them to identify, among the sea of color swatches, just which pink the old family beach house had been painted. On the canvas, each stacking horizontal stripe records the reported memory, and of course none of them are the same. I love the painting for its story, for what it suggests about a group of people all right and all disagreeing. But the collector doesn't smile until he asks me, "You know why I bought this?"

He finishes the answer himself. "There is a saying in the gallery world that no one buys a pink painting. Whatever you think of it in the gallery, you can't imagine it at home and nobody buys. Well"—and here his eyes sparkled—"*I* bought a pink painting."

I don't ask what it's like now that he has it at home, hanging in the bedroom. I don't ask because the point he's trying to make is that he is a collector, not a decorator, and a collector ignores convention. It is, in fact, a point of pride: the collector obeys his own muse.

WHAT VISITOR X HAS NOW IS AN IVORY-BILLED MOUNT attached to a cork base cut to resemble bark. What the museum has now, instead of the ivory-billed specimen they'd had since 1894, is a thin manila folder of documents related to the disappearance. There are memos about the need to increase security, appraisals for the insurance company, notes from other institutions with similar specimens expressing their sympathy and confirming how rarely such specimens become available these days. There is no evidence in the file of any correspondence from Visitor X, but a *Des Moines Register* clipping from 1980, fifteen months after the ivory-billed disappeared, references a letter—and a photograph.

According to Robert Hullihan's article, Visitor X had written to console the museum and its visitors. The bird was fine, Visitor

X explained, well treated and well loved. To prove it, the letter contained a picture of Visitor X, face obscured, holding the ivory-billed, which appeared to be in prime condition. The writer says the photograph is too dark to reproduce in the paper, but I imagine it. I imagine it is a black-and-white picture. I imagine it looks like something from a kidnapping case, the proof of life before a list of demands. But Visitor X asks no ransom.

Visitor X does not make the argument that the museum started it, that a proxy of the museum took this bird from nature, from *life*, and that Visitor X only took the skin from the museum. He does not indict museums, as many have, as storehouses of stolen goods. He raises no objection to the institution at all, does not charge the caretakers with negligence or malfeasance. The taking of the ivory-billed is not framed as a liberation or a protest. It has nothing to do with anyone else, in fact.

No, Visitor X explains the event as something personal, almost wholesome. He felt such a remarkable affinity with the ivory-billed on display, a communion really, that there was nothing else for it: he had to have it. Visitor X admits the bird must have had other admirers, but surely none so ardent—obviously none so committed; in short, none who would benefit so much from its permanent acquisition. It's an interesting notion, the museum as auction, every last item parceled out to the bidder who *needs* it most.

It's also interesting that despite having become a specimen's long-term caretaker, Visitor X still identifies with the museum visitor and not the museum. It's the sacrifice of fellow visitors he acknowledges, their loss. To that point, I can't help but notice that if he'd waited until the end of the exhibition, walked out with the specimen near closing on the very last day, no one but the staff and the occasional researcher would have felt the disappearance any differently than if it had gone back into storage.

AN ARTIST FRIEND REMARKS TO ME THAT LATELY SHE'S BEEN finding her entertainment at an upscale supermarket. It's not just the mise-en-scène of privileged American life that's worth watching, it's the stuff on the shelves. She can't believe there's a product labeled "wild Chilean baby pears." How superlatively exotic. She can't believe how tender and naked and raw the little pear bodies seem. She can't believe there are so many jars—rows and rows of jars, their storage the same as their display. How museum-like it seems: each jar a group of individuals dated and labeled as one type, then preserved in fluid.

I ask her what wild Chilean baby pears taste like. She doesn't know. She only visits. She can't afford to take them home.

I WONDER SOMETIMES IF VISITOR X APPRECIATES THE IRONY of disappearing an endangered bird from an extinction exhibition; one minute there's a mount on display and the next it is wholly inaccessible to the rest of the world. I suspect not. I expect he does not think of loss at all when he thinks of the bird. Rather, I imagine he feels only its presence, the way it fills a place that had been empty.

In the letter, above all, Visitor X is at pains to assure the museum the bird will never be sold. This was not an act for monetary gain. No profit will be made. Visitor X seems to have a rather low opinion of such motives. Yet while his own motivation is offered as assurance that the bird was taken for the purest of reasons, the fact that it will never appear on the market also suggests something that sounds rather sinister: it may never be seen again.

IN ALL THE YEARS I WORKED AT THE PHOTO MUSEUM, THERE were of course many photos I loved, and I loved them for many reasons. There was only one, however, that I ever wanted to own. I knew it the first time I saw it. *Field Museum, Trumpeter Swan, North Dakota, 1891* is an early digital print by Terry Evans. It's part of a series of pictures from the natural history collection at Chicago's Field Museum, and in this picture a swan's neck bends back across its body so that its black beak rests near its daintily crossed black webbed feet. A gauzy shroud wrapped around the middle third of the body holds the neck in place. The light is, this will sound excessive, but I swear the light is quietly transcendent, and the twisted dead bird looks serene. It is printed at roughly life-size, and except for an orange specimen tag and the edge of the table, it is almost entirely white. White in different textures: the light shadows of feathers, the ripples in the shroud, the lift of a corner where one sheet of paper beneath the swan overlaps, almost seamlessly, with a second smooth white sheet.

I saw it first at the art fair on Navy Pier. I was there as a museum employee, sitting with the little row of nonprofit tables outside the main hall, but on breaks I tipped my badge to the guards and browsed the fair booths inside. It wasn't just an aesthetic affinity that made me want to have this picture, or the particular thrill I got every time I thought about this beautiful creature being, miraculously, a beautiful creature *from 1891*.

Maybe moving among things that could be sold planted the idea that this was a thing to own, but more importantly, it was a thing to live with. This was a photograph I could not help but envision already on the wall, not a wall from the place where

I currently lived but a place where I would ideally live, hung over my writing desk like a window, as if its glow and its glory were physical, as if it would flood the room with light.

I did the calculations. Despite a recent promotion from twenty hours a week to thirty, and a one-dollar-an-hour raise, there was no question this photograph was out of my reach. If I stopped eating, if I stopped paying rent and taxes, if I lived on air and never needed to take a bus, it would still be two months' wages to buy it. Sure, I could save a little here and there, but by the time I could afford the price I'd seen, the photograph would have had years to appreciate, and I could see the graph in my mind, how my earnings would never intersect with its appraisal. This seemed familiar enough. I'd spent enough time at galleries with art school kids and museum colleagues to know that the people who loved the work and the people who took it home were not necessarily the same.

So it was kismet, a few years and a few more promotions later, to realize that the museum I was working for had at some point purchased the very picture that had so captivated me. We were, for a time, and in a fashion, to live together after all. Not infrequently did I lift it with white gloves off its storage rack in the vault and escort it out for a print viewing. I remember the weight of the wood and the glass, the pose and posture of the carry. With one hand on each far edge, I had to hold my arms chest-height, wide as the frame and stiff as a waltz. Like that, with nothing touching but glove to frame, I held it close as a partner in a formal dance. And two hours later I'd retrace the steps, glide it back into the vault, and close the door.

THE IVORY-BILLED IS THOUGHT TO PAIR FOR LIFE. OR SHOULD I say *was* thought to? It's hard to pick a tense for something so almost certainly lost, but maybe only slipped beyond the pale of our accounting. It is, however, a simple matter of present tense to say that at the Iowa museum, the ivory-billed are paired, too, in death.

The loss of the ivory-billed mount on exhibition means there are just two ivory-billed specimens left at the museum, one male and one female. The ones that remain are fine specimens, but a decision has been made for their protection never to have them on display. You can make an appointment, if you like; someone will show them to you. But the possibility of a chance encounter is all but extinguished.

There's still plenty to see, mind you, if only you knew to ask. Museums are mostly storage, after all, warehouses of a kind. There are vaults and cold rooms and freezers and all sorts of special rooms your admission won't admit you to. But even in the exhibition hall, what's in the display cases is the tip of the iceberg. The bases of those glass boxes are cabinets fit with drawers, fit with locks you would never notice if you didn't already have the key, the whole structure teeming with more than you see. Some of it is just odd space, filled with folding chairs or shipping boxes or tablecloths. But some cases contain specimen drawers, like dresser drawers in your bedroom, but instead of sweaters filled with skins, piled up on each other like ears of corn, a bushel of one bird species, heads all in one direction.

In some ways, the two ivory-billed skins benefit from their seclusion. There is no light, for instance, to fade their black, black feathers. Both sexes have the long, hard ivory bill, but only the male has the signature red crest, the red feathers the first thing to fade. The individuals in this collection were taken seven years apart, in 1885 and 1892, from Sanford and Old Town, Florida, respectively, where and when they may have had their own mates, long since lost and forgotten to us now. It is also possible this is their only pairing: lying on their sides in an acid-free box, the female on her left wing, the male on his right, a sympathetic symmetry, facing each other forever in the dark.

I ASSUME ONE MORE THING ABOUT VISITOR X. I ASSUME THE ivory-billed was the only thing he ever took. This distinction is important. To take one thing is, perhaps, inspiration. To make a habit of it smacks of nothing more than pathology.

Consider, for a moment, the Blumberg collection. As of 1990, the Iowa bibliomane Stephen Blumberg had liberated—his word—23,600 rare books from at least 268 museums and libraries before a friend sold him out for a $56,000 bounty and the FBI took Blumberg into custody. By any measure, it's the largest book theft in US history. The sheer feat of it is fascinating, the complicated motivations are curious, the fact that the collector became the collected is even a delicious bit of irony. But none of it is awesome or ecstatic or sublime.

I ache to believe there are things in the world that have the power to transform us, and I'm sure at least some of them are housed in museums. Let's be clear: I am not advocating theft. I don't believe one needs to possess a thing in order to be illuminated by it. But I revel in the mere possibility that at any turn we might stumble on something so stunning it takes us out of ourselves for a moment, compels us in some manner, and leaves us changed—leaves us better, I hope. I assume that whatever it was that inspired Visitor X, that magnificent intangible thing is perpetual. I assume Visitor X still relishes the bird. I assume that even now the ivory-billed is lit just so, that the skin itself seems to light the room.

IT LOOKS LIKE A TIGER

THE PRINCIPAL NEVER STOPS BY MY DESK. I HAD AN AUDI-
ence with him on my first day, in his office, and I haven't seen
him since. It was all very formal. We exchanged gifts. And his
guidance for the new job, at least as it was translated, came down
to one sentence. The interpreter swiveled from the principal to
me and said, with the phrasing of a fact, or a christening, or the
casting of a storybook spell, "You are an island of English."

A floating island, perhaps, more like those leviathans mis-
taken for land, bobbing up in twenty classrooms every week,
drifting down the halls, but half the time anchored at my desk,
waiting for seafarers to wash up on my back and catch their
breath and start a fire.

When the students come to my desk, they bring tokens. A
pencil. A box of Pocky. A cell phone charm in the shape of a
turtle. A mirror the size of my palm. They bring CDs and make
sure I know the best boy bands, which K-pop idol I should

swoon for. When the teachers come, the gesture is a snack or a note or a business card. Always the ritual of an offering, like the coin you trade a ferryman before the journey can commence.

Then we share vocabulary questions or plans for the hiking club or work out the logistics of getting to noraebang before the departmental dinner, which songs we should sing and then where I should sit and whom I should talk to and the etiquette that will go unspoken later as I am quietly ushered out before the festivities really get going because I am a woman and a foreigner and the youngest member of the faculty, unmarried even, and each of these facts means there are things I am not supposed to see.

One day a poet pulls up a chair and sits down at my desk. He has brought paper and pens and maps. I think about the great big map halfway up the main stairwell of our school, the size of a storm flag. Right there on the landing, floating between floors, it unseams the planet through the Atlantic. I grew up on the coast of California, but even there I'd never seen the earth flattened so that the Pacific Rim was at its heart rather than its edges, not facing the blank unknown but cupping the center of the world.

Isidore de Seville envisioned existence as a series of concentric spheres. There were four, like the four elemental qualities shaping the substance of the universe, and they were all inhabited: angels in the fiery heavens, then birds in the air, fish in the water, and at the core of things, animals on solid earth. This saint of scholars and the internet mapped it all, all of everything, by density, as if from concrete to ineffable, or the other way around.

The poet draws while he talks, so I will understand.

Japan, it looks like a seal, with a ball on its nose.

The poet speaks quietly, so we won't be overheard.

Korea, it looks like a bunny. But you must never say that. You must say it looks like a tiger, with its arm up like this.

The poet gives me this orientation and no more. He gives me these facts like setting the poles of a compass and leaves nothing else behind. He packs up even the unused paper, and he tucks away his pens. He does not let me keep the drawings. He takes away his maps.

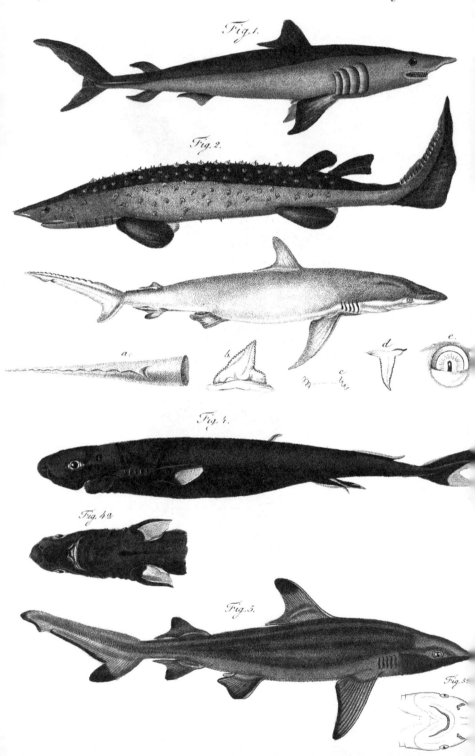

Fig. 1.

Fig. 2.

a. b. c. d. e.

Fig. 4.

Fig. 4.a.

Fig. 5.

Fig. 5.

INTELLIGENT DESIGN

"WHAT KIND OF TAIL DO YOU WANT?" THE TYPE ON THE screen asks me. "What kind of head?"

I make my selections carefully.

I want round eyes instead of beady ones. I pass up the sleek body and choose the curvy one instead. I pick out fins, then teeth. And when it has no more options to offer, the computer assembles all the pieces and displays the result.

"Congratulations!" the screen informs me. "You have made . . . a hammerhead!"

With that, the model pieces fuse together and swim away, leaving a few hammerhead fun facts in their wake. At my console in the aquarium, I stand a little taller. I made something.

Which is strange because I wasn't trying to make a hammerhead. I was just putting bits together in a pleasing way. I was hoping for an exquisite corpse of a shark. I was thinking of the action figures my brother configured once he realized their appendages were only held together with a central rubber band and any arm fit in any socket.

So I try again. I pick the beadiest eyes and the tiniest maw. I take the stubbiest tail and the long, long fins. I refuse to believe that there is a shark for any matrix I might configure, that nature has made a shark for every niche. "This won't work," the computer tells me. "You've matched a predator's eyes with a browser's teeth! It would starve!"

But it doesn't starve. The assembled pieces wiggle, and then they explode. My shark goes *boom*. A two-dimensional cloud billows and fills the screen. When the pixels settle, the type on the screen asks if I would like to try again?

I would. And I stand taller yet as I successfully explode shark after shark, each new combustible breed whole for one shivering moment—and then gone.

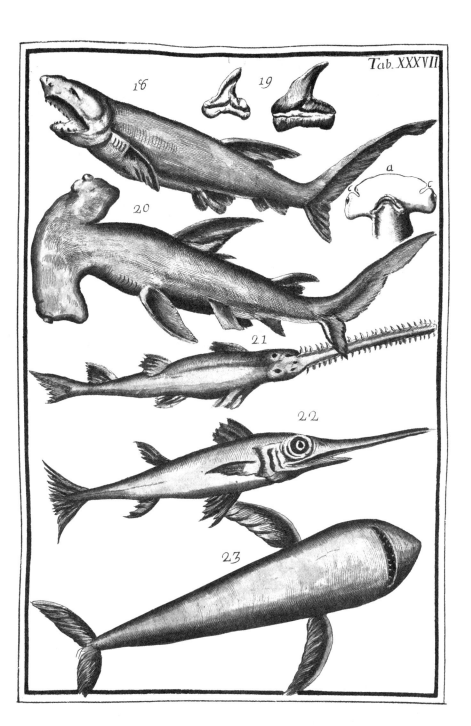

Tab. XXXVII

Real objects are difficult to represent, but the realm of unreal is infinite.

—ZHANG HENG

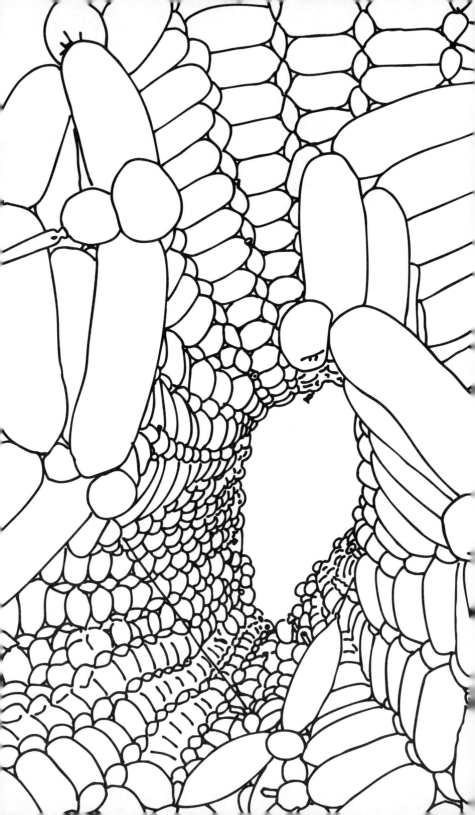

UNTIL IT POPS

WE MET IN THE WANING HOURS OF A WEDDING RECEPTION. IT was dark outside and the musicians had gone home and only the youngish end of the guest list was still up and milling around the first floor of the rented inn when Laura walked up to me to ask, "May I take a picture of your dress? Because I'd like to make it out of balloons."

There is more to say about that evening, about Laura, about how we took a turn about the room reciting lines from *Pride and Prejudice*, how with a clear balloon and a Sharpie she twisted me the story of an invisible *Tyrannosaurus rex* eating the slowest caveman in the history of the world—twisted the whole thing three times because each time I shrieked and laughed so much people came into the room to see what was so diverting and each new audience had to see for themselves just how the wide-eyed caveman head ended up rolling around in the inscrutable belly of the terrible see-through lizard. But this, as much as it can be, is a story about a dress.

Laura is balloon-twisting royalty, elite, an echelon sometimes whispered about in certain circles as the *Balloominati*. She was married in a big white balloon wedding dress twisted by the groom. Which is to say she'd been in such a rig before, but she'd only lately decided to try engineering one herself. And in no time flat, she doesn't just want to make a dress *like mine*, she wants to make a dress *for me*.

A balloon dress entails a solid day or two of labor, but ten minutes into our acquaintance we are already what Laura calls BFFUIPs, and there are things you will do for your *best friend forever until it pops*. Our contract is thirteen words texted into the ether: "I promise I will make you a balloon dress in Chicago in Feb." It is October. We are in California, me back home just for the weekend. An hour ago the police dropped by to warn the party that a bear had been spotted roaming the backstreet, that we should exercise caution, the groom nodding with all due earnestness befitting the situation, though he was wearing a red clown nose just then, had a juggling pin tucked under his arm.

THE 2010 TWIST AND SHOUT, THE ANNUAL BALLOON TWIST-ers' convention, is actually in the suburb of Oak Brook, though the patchy snow and biting air confirm it is February. After three hours of gray-scale landscape and blank highways, holding the first speeding ticket of my life, I know even in the parking lot I have come to the right place. Vehicles everywhere are custom wrapped to convey airbrush artists and face painters and magicians. You wouldn't believe how many personalized balloon-pun license plates there are. I turn the wheel of my anonymous little rental car and settle in next to the green Grand

Caravan of Skiddles the Clown, feeling a bit like I have landed in Oz. At the very least, I'm not in Iowa anymore.

The entrance of the Oak Brook Marriott is staid and impersonal, except for the conspicuous fact of Al Capone's bulletproof 1928 Cadillac sculpted in balloons and amply taking up the lobby. In life the Caddy was 3,500 pounds of steel armor plating and inch-thick glass. In the Marriott it is a mass of latex and air that will start to sag under its own deflating weight by the end of the four-day convention, but for now is jaunty with inflated mobsters spilling out the windows and hanging off the back bumper, brandishing balloon tommy guns meant as welcome, not as threat.

It is already late when I check in, later still when I find Laura, but just early enough to still catch the 11:00 p.m. convention sessions. Laura pulls me into Todd Neufeld's "Twisting for Grown-Ups," into the last back-row seats as the hall fills to standing room only. Laura has brought confections from California and soon I am eating chocolate cupcake from the well of a mason jar with a borrowed hotel spoon. Todd is drinking a brown bottle of Sam Adams, after midnight will switch to a rum imported from Martinique and offer a drink to anyone with a cup to hold it. Randy, everyone seems to know Randy, sips from a flask imprinted with purple balloon dogs as Todd, who years ago quit law school to twist full-time, explains the psychology of a corporate party in three easy steps: Start small. Leave their hands free for drinks. Do one really impressive sculpture and do it at the end.

It's past one in the morning already. Todd is tossing out Tootsie Rolls and shakers of Tic Tacs and one shiny red apple. The audience nods in recognition when Todd says adults don't want balloons—they want an experience, a story, a feeling.

The room is giddy and reverent, a sleepover crossed with midnight Mass.

"Tomorrow," Laura whispers to me without taking her eyes off the speaker. "We'll talk about the dress tomorrow."

• ⁂ •

I ALREADY KNOW WE WILL NOT BE RE-CREATING THE DRESS Laura first saw me in. The thing Laura liked about that blue-green frock was the asymmetrical V neck drawn down to the left into a light cluster of fabric gathered up like paper flowers. The ruffle of blooms would have been doable, but the skirt that starts just below the bust and flares out is a problem. At a balloon dress weekend workshop in Los Angeles, Laura's instructor was sad to say that empire waists simply don't translate into the medium of inflated latex. What flatters in fabric can be just shapeless bulk in balloons. Balloons do not drape. And when you inflate a woman an extra inch all the way around, you still give her a figure. In the world of balloon dresses, size doesn't matter, but silhouette is everything.

"How sexy are you willing to go?" Laura asked me a few weeks ago, a little loud, over the engine noise, having taken my call while driving to a library gig. "I mean, are you willing to show some skin?"

I considered this from an attic apartment I was visiting, bundled up in a long wool cardigan and thick socks, looking out the window at Seattle's unending overcast gray. Usually my sartorial choices have been rather modest. I mean, I'm happy to show off my arms in a tank top and I was once maid of honor in a last-minute silver strapless dress, but I also spend a lot of time under the fluorescent light of dressing rooms pinching up straps with my fingers, wondering if I can take them in enough to bring the neckline closer to my neck. I raced in uniform singlets and short shorts for years, but I've also dressed in locker rooms, even empty ones, with a thin gym towel pinned around my body until the last possible moment, afraid of what teammate or stranger or friend I couldn't say. But when I think about a balloon dress, when I think about someone designing me a dress from scratch—a dress that is a sculpture! a dress that is its own occasion!—I am willing to think differently.

"You can have all the back you want," I said. "The neckline can plunge but I'd prefer it not scoop. I'd like a little warning if you're planning a high hemline. Basically, I want my mother to be able to see these pictures."

No one had ever made a dress for me before. My grandmother made baby blankets. My mother made doll clothes and costumes to transform me for dance class: made me a bear or a purple people eater or the wind. She once labored over a Peter Pan costume, cutting out every leaf from sheets of felt with black-handled shears so I might spin in a sylvan splay of orange oak leaves, yellow elm, red maple, and green ash. I myself bought three yards of yellow-gold silk textured with a pattern of roses in Argentina when I was eighteen, thinking it might be something someday. I bought two meters of pintucked violet satin in Australia a decade later with some similar notion, always planning to fashion myself something but never yet turning out a dress.

Two years before, I was in Brooklyn, staying at a friend's place in Bed-Stuy and telecommuting to my job in Chicago while he went into work in Manhattan. Each morning Earl left me directions to find lunch amid the beauty parlors and discount shops lining Fulton Street, left me detailed instructions on how to order doubles and bakes so I wouldn't be thrown when I had to make a series of decisions not hinted at on the menu board. One afternoon I strayed farther down the street, sailed off the map of my sticky notes, told myself I'd turn around at this stoplight, or the next.

I didn't enter Futa Fashion expecting to walk out with one of the batik-patterned wedding dresses or tie-dyed corduroy sport coats on display in the windows, but they were too enchanting not to go in. The store was dark and spare, each garment hanging with plenty of space and the lights not switched on, like a shop going out of business. Thumbing the racks I found exactly one thing I wanted, a wrap dress with long, gray panels serged together in cords of pink variegated thread, and it fit exactly right. That is, the top fit exactly right. The cap sleeves cupped my shoulders, the front panels crossed without gap and tied neatly at the side. The skirt was a svelte A-line that dropped just below my knees, and everything was perfect right up until the moment I dared to move.

As I studied the mirror, a man walked in, the bells on the door jingling. The tiny middle-aged woman who'd been helping me paid him no mind, but he noticed me, saw the knit in my brow, and stopped behind me. Looking over my right shoulder at the two of us in reflection, his brow wrinkled too. "You don't like it," he said in an accent inflected with French by way of Africa. "It looks good, but you don't like it."

I explained, hesitantly, to this man I did not know, that the wrap opened too much when I walked, the panels gaping to mid-thigh with even a regular stride. I didn't point out that an unexpected gust of wind risked baring the whole leg—maybe more—and he didn't explain his sudden investment in the proper fit of what I was wearing.

"Hmmmm," he murmured in assessment. "You just need more dress."

While I stood dress-less in the stock room, a cramped corridor of sewing machines and loose papers called to serve as the dressing room, Chama called out reassurances. "It's no problem! You'll like it! You'll see!" I could hear the whir of the serge machine on the other side of the wall, its deep hum one noise, one motion as Chama added a new strip of panels to extend the swathe of skirt that wrapped under. It made all the difference. He was right about everything.

The sewing was swift, but it took a long time to ring up the purchase. We talked about the shop, about how Chama started designing, about the fabric he found here and the fabric that came from across the ocean. I walked out an hour later, thrilled with the garment but stunned by a new epiphany. I thought: Why buy a dress, when you can buy a story?

● ⁂ ●

LAURA AND I HAVE BEEN BRAINSTORMING ICONIC DRESSES. We contemplate Bjork's swan dress in balloons. We picture Alice in Wonderland's blue puff-sleeve pinafore puffed into being. We imagine twisting Carol Burnett's green velvet send-up from "Went with the Wind!" and I can so clearly see sweeping into the room with its inflated curtain rod of a yoke.

But the conversation comes in fits and starts. Walking through the Oak Brook Marriott with Laura is like cruising the high school hallways with popular girls in a movie. Every-one knows her and wants to say hi. Laura waves and smiles and makes introductions. Smarty Pants is wearing suspenders. Tawney Bubbles flew in from Vegas. Nate the Great takes my phone and enters his name in my contacts as "ANSWER ME." I meet the inventor of balloon fireworks, then the innovator of Balloon Manor and Elastic Park. Then the Spaniard from Dublin, the Brit from Japan, the balloon dominatrix in from New York. One of them describes Twist and Shout as a family reunion where you actually like the people who show up, and the warmth is so genuine I know it's no mere line.

The day starts at dawn, with TV camera crews and the

whoosh of industrial leaf blowers inflating flat disks that look not unlike giant whoopee cushions. The stated purpose of this spectacle is to set a new record for number of people simultaneously each inside their own giant balloon. Previous record: one.

A six-foot-diameter balloon may have other uses, but mostly it's a finale for professional twisters with no previous history of claustrophobia. Laura does it as a snow globe. Mr. Happy has a specialty yellow smiley face balloon and always wears his smiley face boxers when he performs, knowing firsthand both the distinct risk of being pantsed by the sudden violent contraction of a giant balloon popping, and that it just works out better for everyone if being stripped to your skivvies looks like part of the show.

Twelve participating twisters line the corridor, gripping the necks of their balloons, their arms like the little fuses on cartoon Acme bombs. Each twister is assigned a spotter armed with something sharp.

"The safe word is *pop*," Miss Dena stresses to the spotters.

"That's right," her husband, Smarty Pants, emphasizes, sounding very stern for a man wearing a fez and glasses with no glass to fill the black frames. "Help! Get me out! I'm in a balloon!" can be very funny; maybe it's part of the act. "You don't want to kill the joke," Smarty says. "You don't do anything until someone says *pop*."

The twelve twisters pull the giant balloons on headfirst. They wriggle and shimmy and work the latex maw over each shoulder, down their stomachs, around their hips, push it down to their knees, and step inside. Then, standing astride the entrance like a trapdoor, they reach down and cinch the neck, holding it from the inside. They start to walk, rolling the spheres from within like hamster balls, the fist clutching the nozzle moved along with each step like the tick of a clock hand sweeping up to midnight. Once it is overhead, the twisters begin to hatch, crown, emerge heads out, wearing the nozzles like turtlenecks, and stop there—just heads on latex bodies swollen round as blueberries, like Violet Beauregarde about to leave the chocolate factory, but smiling.

A convention of Catholic school principals has also booked the Marriott, its participants mixing between sessions with twisters in the halls. I jostle with collared priests to get a picture, hold my camera just above a nun's outstretched phone as we all try to capture what cannot last. No one says *pop*.

The day unfolds, reeling from friend to friend while I am initiated to the rivalry of the two major balloon suppliers, familiarized with the retirement and health insurance concerns of the small business owner, and escorted around entries in the sculpture competitions. The sculpture work is painstakingly thought out. In every size category, the entries are by turns funny and virtuosic and macabre. There's a blue-eyed Humpty Dumpty, for instance, tumbling down a balloon brick wall onto the unsuspecting three blind mice. There's a life-size break-dancer, forearms taut and accurately muscled, balanced on one hand. There's a pair of twelve-inch rats, one's neck snapped in a mousetrap, eyes bulging, while the other looks on in horror.

When I am reunited with Laura, she has only two things to say about our pending balloon dress: "Meet me in the Jam Room at ten tomorrow morning." And: "I think you're right about Marilyn Monroe."

TWISTING IS AN INTERPRETIVE ART. IT IS NEVER AIMING FOR simulacrum, does not trade on the uncanny technical verisimilitude of photorealistic paintings or the wax museum. But it does traffic in some vein of facsimile, of essential recognition, of a minimum of cues to complete reference to something known. It's a terribly symbolic medium. A few signs and an icon is invoked. It is not like glass, that astonishing mimic of texture and color and form that can be patently vitreous or dead ringer for something else. There is no latex trompe l'oeil. A balloon sculpture is always, obviously, made of balloons. And yet it is always, obviously, more than that. It *is* Kermit the Frog. It *is* Grandma on a paddleboard. It *is* the precious stolen bonsai tree, just like you asked for. The art of twisting is to channel. It *is* a wall of moms, a billion Elsas, a Texas cat touching snow for the first time. It *is*

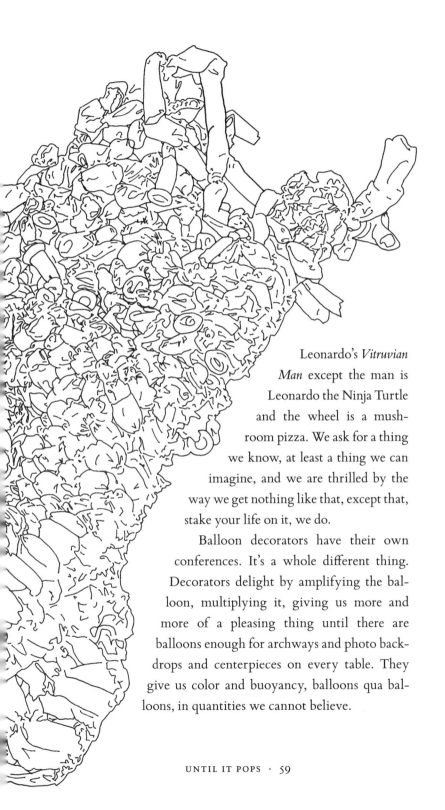

Leonardo's *Vitruvian Man* except the man is Leonardo the Ninja Turtle and the wheel is a mushroom pizza. We ask for a thing we know, at least a thing we can imagine, and we are thrilled by the way we get nothing like that, except that, stake your life on it, we do.

Balloon decorators have their own conferences. It's a whole different thing. Decorators delight by amplifying the balloon, multiplying it, giving us more and more of a pleasing thing until there are balloons enough for archways and photo backdrops and centerpieces on every table. They give us color and buoyancy, balloons qua balloons, in quantities we cannot believe.

But balloon twisters do something else. Twisters delight almost by turning the balloon against itself, defying it, subverting it, court the delight that it is possible to make *that* out of balloons. If decor is pleasure, twisting is desire. It's a very human act to make an object a vessel. It is such a commonplace way to make meaning, so very part of the ether, as to become invisible. How supremely satisfying and surprising and remarkable that our desires can—in some ways *must*—be pulled out of thin air.

● ⁝ ●

THE JAM ROOM IS SORT OF THE BEATING HEART OF TWIST AND Shout. Functionally, it's a center of research and development, all craft and chance encounter, the vibe somewhere between sewing circle and all-you-can-eat buffet. It occupies the Marriott's whole Prince of Wales Ballroom. Rival companies Betallic and Qualatex alternate days supplying the goods, and twisters are welcome to all the balloons they can inflate.

You could get lost there. You could fall down the rabbit hole and lose track of time and forget to come out. Indeed, some twisters skip the rest of the convention altogether and just buy day passes to the Jam Room. Ten tables end to end support a gapless stretch of boxes offering eighty running feet of everything the balloon world has to offer. They are organized in a matrix of size and shape—tubes and spheres, hearts and toroids—but it's the spectrum of color that's stunning. Decide to twist a bullfrog, say, and you have to decide if it's Crystal Green, Neon Green, Metallic Green, Metallic Turquoise Green, Metallic Key Lime, Deluxe Key Lime, or Fashion Forest Green.

Twisters of all ages, at all hours, pull up chairs in loose clusters, kicking their way through failed unicorns and limbs loose from their junctures to puzzle out a better Daffy Duck. The Jam Room is open continuously, and there are always people inside.

The balloon dress is going to take hours. Laura has settled on a hard deadline of 8:00 p.m., the start of the end-of-conference banquet, but is hoping to finish early so she has time to get ready herself. Nobody mentions Laura is sometimes, professionally, a fairy godmother, that she has the wand at home. "We can do this," she tells me. "If we're smart about it." And if I can help.

Laura is an accomplished performer, but twisting balloon couture is a recent addition to her wheelhouse. This is the first dress she will ever make—so far, we are equal. Then Laura pulls up two hotel banquet chairs, sits me in one and a heavy leather box in the other.

"Have you ever used one of these?" she asks. I understand the flexible black tube snaking up into a brass nozzle head. I recognize the rumble of an air compressor switched on. I want to ask how on earth she got this thing through the airport—have heard marvelous stories about twisters interrogated about their gear only to leave the TSA checkpoint with security smiling and wearing funny hats. Instead I try to remember the last time I inflated my bike tires at a gas station.

I say, "Let's assume no."

But faster than I can reference Lady Catherine de Bourgh's "If I had ever learnt, I should have been a great proficient," my left hand is slipping balloons on the nozzle, the index finger of my right hooked through the brass loop and steady on the trigger. *Ggbbbrrrrrrrr* the pump rumbles again and again, and each time a limp length jerks up into a sprouting tusk.

The actual dress in *The Seven Year Itch* was made in ivory so that on screen it would read as white. The designer called it "bone." Laura wanted to do our dress in Pearl, but somehow the Qualatex rep doesn't have enough of the special-run color, so we are using White. Specialty balloons are sized by their diameter and length in inches. A 260, for instance, the standard choice for your run-of-the-mill one-balloon balloon dog, is two inches in diameter and sixty inches long when fully inflated. Dressmakers, spinning straw into gold as they are, favor the proportions of the smallest of standard sizes: the 160. The comparatively narrow diameter allows for the shortest twists and smallest bubbles, balloon dresses made by weaving a warp and weft from these nonetheless chunky, squealing, weightless threads.

It takes me two hours to inflate two hundred Qualatex White 160s. It's long enough my fingers are sore, long enough that I've ceased to jump, or even look up, at the periodic *bang* of burst balloons throughout the Jam Room. The standard adjustable dress forms are in use by the two other dressmakers, so Laura's off shopping the vendors for an inflatable form. She has been gone so long I begin to wonder if she could just as easily have twisted one, when she shows up, breathless, with a retractable stand and two limbless, headless, blow-up trunks. There is something unsettling about these naked torsos, how casually they topple in the waste of lost balloons, breasts poking up from a disposable mess of false starts and abandoned efforts. Laura retrieves one as my proxy, screws the chosen form onto a stand, and tells me to come back in a few hours.

•　⁂　•

WILLIAM TRAVILLA DESIGNED THE MOVIE DRESS BONED WITH metal so the halter neck would stay flat against the skin. In interviews afterward he seemed flustered, angry even, that something so common was getting so much attention. The object was made with all due technical skill, of course, made both to shine on screen and to withstand the wear and tear of production, but this dress was just a prop, less a flight of fancy than an echo, an adaptation, a dress that was vulgar in the sense that it was already popular, vernacular, a style that had already caught on.

Laura's creation is nothing but balloons, so she needs my actual neck to make sure the halter straps tie together at the right length, but mostly all I can do now is chat with whoever has come to keep her company as she weaves. The bodice keeps growing longer but the skirt is forever suggested only by the fringe of warp strand balloons, a splay of wild sea-witch tentacles, whipping every which way. I start to wish we were weaving Pearl Onyx Black and that I'd used my voice to ask for Ursula. Instead, looking at its gradual progress, I am increasingly aware of my legs.

At 6:00 p.m. Laura has just gotten to the skirt proper. By 7:00 it begins to ripple. By 7:30 it's clear the hem will not make it to the standard-bearer's mid-calf as intended, but Laura hustles me upstairs with what looks like a quiver of White 160s over my shoulder and the dress form tucked under my arm. The dress already represents a good ten hours of twisting. With another two, the hemline would be accurate, but we don't have another two. Kenwyn, the balloon dominatrix from New York, knocks on the door as promised and comes in to tie me off.

Laura fumbles with the button system to open the dress while I slip out of the charcoal corduroys and ash-gray shirt I've been in all day. Laura twists in some coverage where the halter meets the bodice. Kenwyn twists and ties a pretty hem of short and long bubbles repeating, *dit-dah dit-dah dit-dah*, like a continuous "AAAAAAAA" screamed in Morse code. I stand between them, my arms raised like a music box dancer, frozen while they work. At almost any other point in my life this scrutiny and proximity would have mortified me. But I appreciate, maybe for the first time, here in the Marriott, these two things: I am safe with these women, and no one really cares.

I manage to get one of my shoes on all by myself, but it's just easier if Laura buckles the other one. When I fold to reach my feet, the bubbles at the waist strain and the skirt springs up like some petticoat sight gag and I can't see what I'm doing. A stage combat instructor once taught me that if you fall and your legs go up in the air, we know it's comedy, but lie flat and we know it's serious. By that measure this unruly, unsinkable dress is not in any way serious, even if by wearing it I join a long line of women fitted in garments someone else had to put them in. So much attire serves to hobble us. So much is meant to make us more.

• ⁂ •

WHEN WE USE *DRESS* AS A VERB, WE SOMETIMES MEAN TO clothe, as in attire. We sometimes mean to bind, as in bandage. And we sometimes mean to gut, as in butcher. Imagine: one word for both raiment and slaughter.

• ⁂ •

MARILYN MONROE WORE TWO PAIRS OF UNDERWEAR TO BE sure the one hundred official photographers and up to five thousand onlookers awake on Lexington Avenue and Fifty-Second Street in the wee hours of September 15, 1954, wouldn't see more than she wanted in the course of three hours and fourteen takes. The tights I have on hand, black, patterned with flowers and vines, thematically make no sense, but what matters is they are opaque. Laura architects the gravity-defying skirt to sit lower with some creative rigging to tether its great sweeping ripples to one another. And then that's it. We've run out of time. Everything will turn into a pumpkin. It's not our ideal, but it's enough. The reference is unmistakable.

Laura says you can sit on balloon dresses, that the pressure distributes evenly and nothing pops. But there's no convincing yourself this should be true, and it's not worth sitting down if you are distracted the whole time imagining disaster. Most balloon dress models stand. At the banquet I can spot the other balloon dresses because their wearers stand for two hours straight in unyielding sheaths. One is a pinnacle of blue, the other a beacon of every color.

My skirt, however, is so full and lively it can, discreetly no less, be manipulated with nothing revealed as I take a seat next to a man wearing balloon cuff links at banquet table 12. Should anything happen to the dress, Laura has sent me off with three replacement balloons like so many spare tires. I like to imagine them sewn in along a seam, like extra buttons, but instead they're clustered in the middle of the table like a stand of marshmallow cattails.

The banquet is a whole show, and at intermission, a man approaches me, says, "Not that I was looking, but you have a few popped balloons." He pauses as I consider their possible locations. "Okay," he says, leaning in, "I was looking."

For a place full of comedians, I'd expect a better joke. I lose him in a flurry of photographers, of posing alone or with strangers, and I never do find popped places. A laughing woman takes her picture with me, laughs again and slides a balloon flower ring with white petals off her hand and onto mine, says it goes with my outfit, and disappears in the crowd.

The banquet ends, but the photo shoot continues anywhere I take the dress. In the sculpture hall I ask for my own picture with the bronzy, life-size, natural-history-style *Spinosaurus* skeleton towering above me. I admire again the work of hundreds of uninflated balloons rolled into pointillism tribute to *A Sunday on La Grande Jatte—1884*. The original was decried as "scandal" and "hilarity" when unveiled, and the technique employed in this version, too, has proved controversial.

The official judging over, the competition is now pure exhibition. The guys who made a pink Cadillac have climbed onto its balloon bench seat for their own photo op. Presumably their sculpture is not in honor of Elvis Presley's first pink Cadillac, left in flames on the roadside three months after purchase, but his second Fleetwood Series 60, purchased a little later in 1955, the iconic one painted a custom "Elvis Rose" and given to his mother—never mind she never had a driver's license and it was Elvis behind the wheel.

These twisters, ensconced in their own creation, exaggerated in pantomime, pretend to honk the fake horn when I walk past. It's a funny coincidence, these two kinds of star vehicle, two idols of 1955 invoked in ephemera and colliding in a Marriott half a century after the fact. I walk on, out of the way, and I can't tell if it's clever or bad behavior, this silent catcall, this moment of one icon hailing another.

•　✺　•

LATEX, FROM THE LATIN FOR "LIQUID," IS PRODUCED UPON injury. It is not sap or milk, can be clear or yellow, or orange or red, but is usually exuded as white. It is present in some 10 percent of flowering plants, as well as some mushrooms and conifers, one of those products of convergent evolution, selected for again and again. And though we make mattresses and swim caps and catheters from some of its varieties, chewing gum and opium from others, wrap up the world in rubber bands and rub it out with erasers, the value of latex in nature appears to be defense. Botanist Joseph F. James described in 1887 "such disagreeable properties that it becomes a better protection to the plant from enemies than all the thorns, prickles, or hairs that could be provided." Caterpillars, in great numbers, die trapped in stickiness as it clots.

•　✺　•

NOW THAT I AM HABITAT FOR THIS DRESS, THE MOST NOTICE-able thing is the static electricity. Like when you rub a party balloon against the fabric of your shirt and then bring it near your head to make the hair stand on end. Except this is happening to every hair on my arms. I am prickled in fine spikes. I have a force field and an electric aura. I am a tribute to tension, to pressure and volume, all ions and charge, poised to attract or repel. I feel like a force of nature. Touch me and I crackle and snap. But even in the physics of it, there is no real protection.

I meet Laura at the hotel bar, and the man referred to as the Irish Spaniard, mugging for a picture, sidles up and puts his hand on the balloon panel over my left breast. I know this because I see it, because he does it to be seen. But I can't feel his hand at all through the tension of an inch of air, not his skin or clammy palm, not the pressure of the grope. It is so diffused, the force of his hand. For all I know, it is lightly done. Surely so, if he means to touch an image and not a real thing.

This should perhaps make it a lighter trespass, less harm done, but without the sensory shock to distract me, the sheer symbolic act is impossible to ignore. It is an act of such naked entitlement, such raw objectification, artlessly repeating under the guise of humor basic can't-you-take-a-joke assault. Yeah, yeah, yeah, he doesn't mean anything by it. Only, it doesn't mean any less once it is stripped down to only meaning.

Marilyn Monroe's character in the movie, as in the play that preceded it, is credited as "The Girl." Like "The Plumber" or "Waitress at Vegetarian Restaurant" also in the script, except more generic, more anonymous, perhaps more universal. "The Girl" is an employed, adult person who moves to New York, but the plot means to revolve around Richard Sherman, who lives in the apartment below hers, and from his reference she is only The Girl. Even The Girl's rayon-acetate crepe gown, with its rolled hem and every pleat formed by hand and sewn into place, was referred to by its designer as "that silly little dress." Its fame embarrassed him. He wanted to be known for his more impressive feats. As wardrobe, that dress has to illustrate the temptations of The Girl's neighbor, and yet its essential narrative point is to communicate her innocence.

I am the age Marilyn Monroe was when the movie premiered. I was the age she was during filming when I discovered my own windswept grate. You could stumble on it, too, right there next to the Iowa River, on the kind of cold winter day where everything is pulled into your parka and clenched, hat yanked down to your lashes, hood cinched, scarf wrapped until there is just the slit of your squinting eyes watering in the frozen air. You might make out a patch of steam rising from the sidewalk, but more likely all you'll see is a thawed spot in the ice made by the continuous vent of warm air. It is an oasis. It gives you a moment to gather yourself, to recover, to open your eyes and see a world you don't actually recognize because its very conditions mean you never have comfort or time or perspective enough to take it in.

I thought this balloon dress would be clever and charming. I mean, how right to reinterpret an object made an icon entirely because of the way it was animated with air! How funny to freeze a famously fluid dress into a static, squeaky form! But now that I am in the dress and not the abstract, it feels like I have called forth something I did not know would be bidden, channeled a force too great for one person to wield.

Despite all the hours and all the takes done on site, the famous subway grate scene in the movie was shot later on a Hollywood lot, where it was easier to control the sound, though the publicity shots they used were the ones on location. Monroe's husband was on set at the scene's New York filming, apparently persuaded by a gossip columnist to attend. You'd like to think that as another celebrity of the era, he'd have been sympathetic to the situation, its demands, but the crew remarked on his dark and worsening mood. The director said he had "the look of death." The scene wrapped, and back at their hotel room the couple fought. The altercation was referenced soon after in their divorce proceedings. Some accounts call it a fight. Some say she was "bruised." Some report she was beaten so badly she couldn't work for a week.

• ᛫ •

WE TALK ABOUT PERSONAL SPACE AS A BUBBLE, LIKE THOSE six-foot balloons, which are still so perilous as to need a safe word. In this dress I have a visible, literal bumper. I have an inch of buffer marked between me and the world that starts where the balloon dress ends. It seems like that should matter. But I was better off in a cotton tee. I cannot for the life of me figure out if the dress has transformed or negated me, if I am one with it like a plastic figurine or if I am merely scaffolding to be ignored, like the pole holding up an illuminated sign, so bright, so tempting, begging you to stop.

Not a soul had been untoward when I was just another person wearing a conference lanyard. In no other context have I seen someone touch another twister's sculpture without permission, just like no one at the banquet attempted to take food off my plate. But somehow this balloon dress, this intersection of what reads as balloon and dress and body and icon, somehow it becomes a category of its own. Spun in bespoke bubble wrap, I am not extra protected. I feel all but canceled out. Never have my boundaries been so transparent, both obvious and transgressed.

I've had enough. I can see that this dress—just the *idea* of this dress—attracts more than I care to shoulder. It's like wearing a lightning rod. It's like I have invoked something, summoned it, called it down without bracing for it to hit. I walk towards the elevator, towards the promise of my corduroys and a wool sweater, when the banquet's official comedian, now off stage and a few sheets to the wind, staggers to intercept me. There is no particular audience to perform for between the bar and the elevator bank. The lighting is bad. He tries clumsily, half-heartedly, to lift up my skirt. It's almost perfunctory. His face is more stupor than leer. He peaks his eyebrows sleepily as if to say, "I had to try," as if to shrug, "Whatta ya gonna do?" As if it were the custom, as if neither of us could help it, as if it were just a box to tick. He cannot be bothered with showmanship. I cannot suspend my disbelief.

LATEX IS BIODEGRADABLE. GIVEN TIME, IT WILL DECAY AND disintegrate and return to the earth. For an inflated latex balloon to live the longest possible life, you put it in a plastic bag and place it in a freezer. The trunk of a car during a Midwest winter is not such a bad substitute. The sprawling dress survives the drive home beautifully. How fragile I assumed it was, how delicate and fleeting. I wondered if the coarse upholstery fibers might prick it. I've heard grass is the great enemy of balloons, second only to the children themselves, and I could imagine so many ways it could burst. I gave no thought to how it might persist.

I hang it on a doorknob, and for weeks it withers. It loses its scent of latex. Its squeak turns to a rustle turns to a drag. At first it shrinks a little, as if being taken in, then as if to fit a child. The balloons are woven at different intervals, bubbles twisted between one and four inches long, different ratios of volume and surface area deflating at different rates. The tight weave of the chest contracts first, pulls apart into a latex net, like the thick knobs of crochet. The long tubes of the halter slowly go flaccid. Some bubbles in the skirt lose their air entirely, go thin though still pulled taut, twangy like rubber bands. Nothing pops. It does not explode any more than it becomes a vacuum, is all whimper and no bang as the weak spots give and the knots loosen and it deflates to air pressure equilibrium. The last skirt bubbles begin to pull away from each other, wane thin as fingers, white and rattling as bones.

A year later, I pack it at the top of a Bankers Box, still afraid it could be crushed. By then it is little more than a latex handkerchief, shrunk to dolls' clothes, in texture and scale increasingly reminiscent of those lumpy rainbow pot holders I loomed as a child. I could put it in a shadow box, like a christening gown, if one were going to be baptized by air. Briefly I think of debutantes, of wedding gowns and prom dresses worn for one momentous night and put in storage. Mostly I live my life. I buy other dresses and other stories. I leave this one tucked away. Mostly I don't think about it. But every so often I remember it's still there, still with me, somewhere in the dark, though I haven't seen it, haven't felt it, haven't brought it out for years.

THE TWO TIMES YOU MEET THE DEVIL

THE FIRST TIME I MET THE DEVIL, I WAS WALKING DOWN A steep dirt road, with a friend, the road so steep it had taken five tries in our tiny rental car to maintain enough nerve and momentum, charging towards the decision point of a brick wall, to overcome the slope and still, cranking the wheel, take a harrowing narrow turn that was both sharp and blind. There was no other way. I don't know how we managed. We knew mostly the failed attempt, the near miss, the tires at some intermediate spot churning pointlessly to a stall and slipping us back to where we'd started.

Our success in ascending had been so arduous and unlikely that my friend and I assumed we would never drive up the hill again, that we were on foot now, that we would forsake the vehicle where it was at the summit until we left Tilcara for good. We were walking down the hill, for the first time, still startling, the soles of our shoes slipping a little, too, and our hands periodically flung out to brace, when an old man waved us over.

The old man's clothes were the color of the dirt road. He was missing some teeth. He had a lot to say, a lot of questions to ask, and we understood not a word. It had been a long time since I'd lived in this part of the world, and it seemed reasonable my tongue was clumsy, unable to say what it wanted, my ear cottoned, unable to parse words I should have known, but my friend was a translator by profession and having the same luck. When we could make no sense of his questions, we tried our own, but neither did the old man understand us.

It was then that a young man came up the road to meet us. The young man was handsome, had a beautiful smile, was missing a few teeth too. The young man said, "You'll never guess what I have in my bag."

The bag was about the size of a backpack, big enough to hold a basketball, a few loaves of bread. It would, the thought flashed before me, perfectly cradle a severed human head.

"It's an animal," I volunteered, and the young man laughed.

"No," he said gamely, happily, egging on the next bet.

"In that case," I said, joking back, "it must be *two* animals."

"No," he said, suddenly stern, annoyed, no longer laughing. He added, I assume both to underline his disappointment in my paltry imagination and to definitively put an end to this feeble line of inquiry, "It's not animals."

This was unfortunate. I had not expected, say, a bag full of kittens, but a creature of some kind still seemed one of the better possible outcomes among things that would fit in a gleeful stranger's bag. But there was no puppy, no tiny baby goat, no pangolin curled tight in a ball. Nothing like that at all.

Now the young man was serious. Now the young man was done with guessing and games. He opened his bag in one motion, and there was such a profusion of colorful cloth, so many tiny mirrors stitched to the fabric, that my next guess was a circus tent.

"No," the young man said, his enthusiasm returning. "This is my devil suit."

The devil smiled. The devil was proud of this suit.

"Then why aren't you wearing it?" I asked the devil.

The devil explained, "I only wear it when I'm in town."

He was magnanimous now. The devil assured us, not to worry, he would put the suit on again that evening, when it was time to go back to town. It seemed the devil was needed only in town—and mostly at night—and though we were still arguably in town, within the old city walls if not the new ones,

this particular spot where we'd met was perhaps far enough from the center, maybe just dusty enough or merely part of an old reckoning, not to count. From where we were standing, we could see the mountains, the main road that had brought us here from the seven-colored hills. We could not yet hear the music played in town. It was not quite time to tie flowers to the llamas and parade them through the streets.

The old man, who had said nothing while the devil spoke, now reached out to stroke my hair. Even the devil found this odd, uncomfortable. I saw it in his eyes. Without excusing ourselves, my friend and I briskly resumed our walk down the dirt road and into town. The old man may be there still, for all I know. The devil moved sprightly on his way.

THE SECOND TIME I MET THE DEVIL, I WAS THE ONLY employee of a new bookstore that was already about to fail. It was summer. It was the afternoon. The bookstore was a brick building on a corner lot and the sun streamed through the south and west windows and everything glowed. There was an old leather couch in the middle of the room, its surface cracked and breaking, and I liked to imagine that it was plotting its escape, gradually departing on the legs of customers who sat too long, the bits of couch now fugitive freckles sweat-stuck to the backs of their thighs.

The month before, a man in recovery had come into the bookstore, a basket on his arm, selling banana bread that reeked of the plastic wrapped around each loaf. He was telling me about the ministry he was raising money for, the good works they did, and I couldn't tell him that I actually hadn't been paid in a while. I thought so hard about whether I could afford to give this man five dollars, of what it might mean to him versus what it might mean to me, that when I tried to speak to him, I sobbed.

The man from the ministry was not embarrassed by me. He was gentle. He seemed prepared for this. I wondered later how often it happened, how often someone was asked for something so small and they broke. The man from the ministry set down his basket and asked if he might pray.

I was standing in the very same spot the day the devil walked in. The devil announced himself immediately.

"I am the devil," the devil said.

The devil had little to say about his origins, but he confirmed that he had been the devil for quite some time. What that entailed, it seemed, was in flux. Sometimes he got seasonal work in haunted houses. Sometimes he led tours. Foreigners, he said, foreigners especially like a tour led by the devil. At present the devil was emcee for a monthly circus burlesque, themed on the seven deadly sins, and it was in that capacity that the devil had come into my bookstore to acquire door prizes to award the audience that night.

The devil preferred to buy local, he said. The devil could have spent his money anywhere, I considered, but here he was, trying to keep it in the neighborhood.

I found I had no shortage of books to recommend to the devil. There were many independent presses I thought he might like, several specific titles. The devil had broad tastes, and he was careful in his consideration, appreciative there was so much literature in translation. He read from everything I brought him and, mindful of his audience, finally settled on a thin volume of drawings, crude in both style and subject, and funny as they were dark.

The devil was nothing but patient as I mustered up something resembling gift wrap. We had never gotten around to ordering it, could never justify the expense, so I did what I could with scraps of good paper and a rubber stamp. He didn't mind. The devil seemed to have all kinds of time.

He talked at length about neighborhood history and photography and music he liked. He suggested I come by the burlesque some night. And all that time I was with the devil, no other customers walked in. No bits of shattered couch attached themselves to depart on the back of his black jeans. After I had done all I could with the wrapping, I handed the devil the thing he had come for, and the devil paid in cash.

I USED TO THINK I COULD NOT WRITE ABOUT THE DEVIL— not until we met for a third time. There's rhetoric in threes, I thought. *Meaning.* Three is the difference between coincidence and a pattern. The number seemed to matter. I mean, isn't the devil like that?

It's not that I've since grown impatient. And it's not that I've despaired of meeting him once more. It's just I've come to think it doesn't matter.

The devil, in these encounters, had been very forthcoming. It's charming, I think: the devil in broad daylight, the devil running errands, the devil so delighted he cannot keep his joy to himself. Does that not have meaning of its own? I love the way the devil announces himself. How disarming! And it's these times I've met the devil, these times he's introduced himself, that led me, for a while, to assume that that is how it is. That that is how it always is.

But the more I think about it, the more I wonder how many times we have met, crossed paths at least, exchanged a look, and the devil has said nothing. Isn't the devil like that, too?

SACK OF GRAVEL

THE LEDGER OF MY BODY IS WRITTEN ON THE RIGHT-HAND
side. It starts, I think, with the puncture scars on my right bicep
from the first time our family dog lunged and broke the skin.
Then the longer slice scars along my jaw from the next time,
still in third grade, when he went for my face.

There's the scar down my right wrist the size of a French cuff
buttonhole, from playing in the sawdust on the hillside where
our house was being built: how strange, that injury I could see
but never felt, even as I washed the flap of skin clean in the
kitchen sink. Then there are the scars on my right elbow, shiny
when they flex, all that skin scraped away against asphalt when
the runner ahead of me fell and I followed, all of us only far
enough past the County Championships starting line to have
picked up speed, my right arm and thigh still bleeding when I
crossed the finish line three miles later, loosely bandaged as I sat

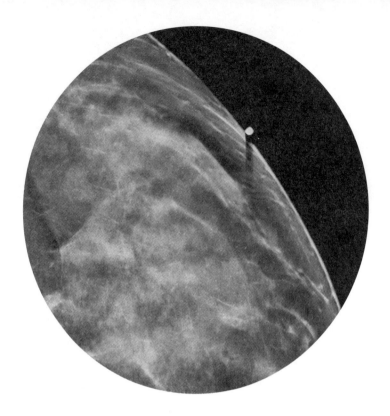

shivering in an emergency room that evening, waiting to rule out concussion.

Next it's the right thumb, scarred at the joint from bottle-feeding a baby boar while I worked at the zoo in Santiago. And the soft focus of my right eye, the one that needed correction first, in college, that curve of lens held in the frame of my glasses discernibly thicker than its neighbor even now. Also, the thin-walled molar, lower right, more filling than tooth, that the dentist on the avenue insists must hurt all the time, must drive me to distraction, must keep me up at night sucking at a pain I insist I do not feel. Add to that three stitches on my right side, like legs on an ant, where a Chicago doctor excised a mole from my waist. And the right ear I couldn't hear through for a time in Greece. The right ankle I twisted so badly, having missed the last descending stair of my favorite Iowa apartment, that the whole

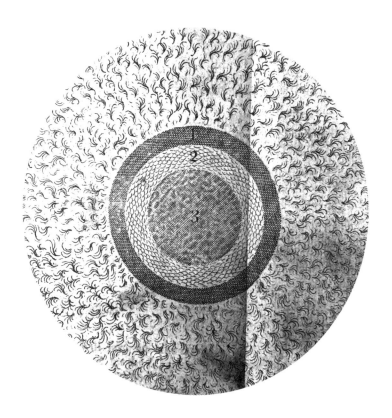

foot bruised purple black, a ring like I had stepped into a shallow dish of ink, except it was blood pooled beneath the skin.

Now there's the right knee that's beginning to twinge, sometimes gives, when I take the stairs. And the tender soreness in my right heel, especially when I wake, that reminds me not just that I have walked too far the day before but fundamentally how it is that I stand, how I rest, how I shift my hips and my spine and the tilt of my head, without thinking, to carry my weight on the right side.

True, I should note, there's the chicken pox scar just left of center, my first scar, a hollow on the brow ridge where, home from school in my parents' bed, I dared to itch at it, though I had been told not to, until that disk of cells unexpectedly lifted away unattached, a thing and not just a mark, as if I had brushed away a stray piece of confetti that left a divot in its place.

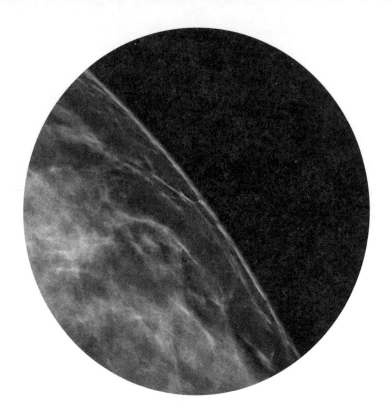

But everything else, every site of compromise and collision that left a mark, all of it has been borne starboard, stage right, on the side of this body faster to block, to flinch, to curl and tense in preparation for the blow. Everything, except for my left breast, which I'm told is a sack of gravel, and which I should mention is beginning to hurt.

•

THE FIRST LUMP WAS THE SIZE OF A PINTO BEAN. THAT WAS the language of my doctor. I called it Pinto, because she had, though I defaulted to imagining it as a lima, something broad and pale and bigger than it was. I knew perfectly well the difference between soupy soft pinto beans on a Tex-Mex plate and the hard ones scooped and poured and scooped up again in plastic cups in preschool, their smooth resistance if you ran

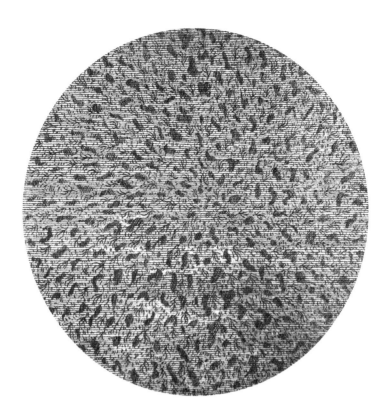

your fingers through the sack. But the lump was not familiar, had nothing to do with what I knew about pinto beans, so I did not think about whether it was cooked or dried or growing in a field. Instead it came to mind as an altogether different bean, an alien bean, a bean I'm not sure I've ever actually seen, have never put into my mouth.

· ·

I DID NOT KNOW THAT SOFTBALL-SIZED HAIL WAS A REAL thing until I moved to Texas and a storm of them totaled cars and shattered roofs and broke the arm of our apartment manager when she ran outside to save her dog. As a modifier, it sounded so colloquial, so impossible, so clearly in the aggrandizing family of fish stories as not to be believed. I did not know until after that storm—not until there was a souvenir stashed in the freezer to remind me it was real—that *softball-sized* was in fact a technical term, nearly the last of a standard set of comparisons used by the US government's meteorologists.

I am still surprised that we use modern, manufactured things to talk about the natural world. Penny and Ping-Pong. Marble or mothball. DVD when grapefruit is not enough. Collectively, the hail terms tend to the sporting—golf ball–sized hail, tennis ball–sized hail—but teacup stands out to me. Partly for its delicacy, its sheer likelihood to be the thing to *break* and not the thing doing the breaking. Partly because I cannot stop myself from picturing the only one left from my grandmother's set: clover pattern with a high loop handle and a flute flared lip. And partly because it seems worth noting that there exists a unit of measure employed to describe the relative size of both poodles and balls of ice.

• • •

MY PREGNANT FRIENDS HAVE APPS ON THEIR PHONES TO TELL them how big the fetus is from week to week. It's a kumquat. It's a plum. The partner of one such friend points out that, early on anyway, the division of cells is so incredibly regular, entirely predictable, that it would make more sense to compare apples to the size of a fifteen-week fetus than the other way around.

I don't disagree. Of course the language of the body should be mixed up with the language of the garden, of husbandry, of the ways we've found to talk about the unruly variance of organic matters.

I did not at the time question the language of my pinto bean, did not ask what it might be next. When the insurance would not cover the mammogram as "routine," the staff typed in a different code whose array of characters they did not bother to pronounce, could not say aloud, shared only that it meant too young for a routine mammogram. They hinted it would cost me. "Abundance of caution," my doctor said.

• • • •

MY DOCTOR DEMONSTRATES THE CIRCULAR PATTERN OF the self-exam, the pressure of two fingers traveling predictably, methodically, like "Ring around the Rosie," like sweeping for a mine. Pinto is my landmark, my planted flag. I'm to call her if it gets bigger, if it changes in any way, if there is anything else that becomes *that big*. I tell her that it's hard to tell the difference, to remember what was there last month, that I never feel like I am doing it right. She assures me it's not that difficult. I promise her I'll do my best.

• • • • •

I DON'T KNOW IF I'M DOING ANYTHING RIGHT. ANYTHING AT all. I am aware of my failures. I am aware that any one of them might kill me.

• • • • • •

MY PARTNER FAILS TO LOCK THE CAR DOOR AND SOMEONE steals our jar of meter change and a box of candy left over from the movies, the sugar shells crushed brightly on the sidewalk. The next time it happens, they basically toss the joint, papers everywhere, napkins and handbills and all the registration slips and insurance cards since my grandparents owned the car. My partner fails to lock the apartment door one night when I am out of town and awakes to the creak of the door opening, of a stranger letting himself in. I have resigned myself to the fact that I will be the one to make sure our doors are locked, the lids are screwed on or snapped tight so the food doesn't spoil, the oven is turned off after a meal is made and the knobs haven't

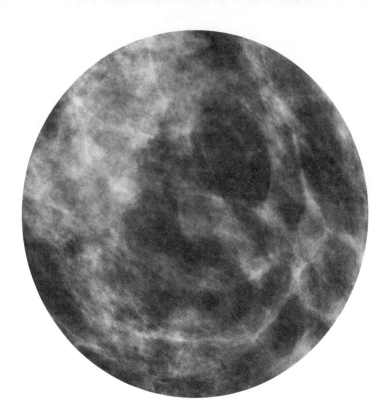

been bumped to release gas so that it seeps without the spark to ignite. I know how to do all this. I don't mind. These are things I can see to do that keep us safe.

$$\bullet \quad \bullet \quad \bullet \quad \bullet \quad \bullet \quad \bullet \quad \bullet$$

I AM ON A PIECE OF BUTCHER PAPER, OR MAYBE DOCTORS' offices call it something else, but anyway that white roll of paper so thin it makes a crinkly noise whenever you move, sticks to the skin where there isn't the veil of the hospital gown to intercede. It is the kind of paper that makes me think of tables protected from the mess of art projects, of slabs and slices wrapped up at the deli and taken home.

I am prone on that paper, in my doctor's new office at the university, in one of the examination rooms, the gown untied and pointless, when she says my left breast is a sack of gravel.

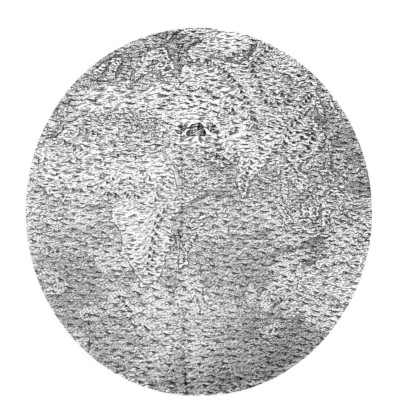

I spend a lot of time in the examination room of my doctor's new university office staring at the art on the wall. I think
about how it might have been chosen, if it will ever change
now that it is installed, whether it's supposed to soothe me. I
can't tell you what the subject is, flowers maybe, though it's
obvious when I'm looking at it. I know they are framed, these
pieces of art, isolated like that. And I would guess that there
are three pictures in the exam room, some number that makes
the walls seem spare, a quantity that seems calculated not to
overwhelm.

Note that my doctor does not use the simile, does not say
my breast is *like* a sack of gravel. She says it *is* a sack of gravel.
Even as she says it, in that space of breath before another word
can be said, it strikes me, I distinctly remember this thought,
that she could hardly have picked a comparison more stripped

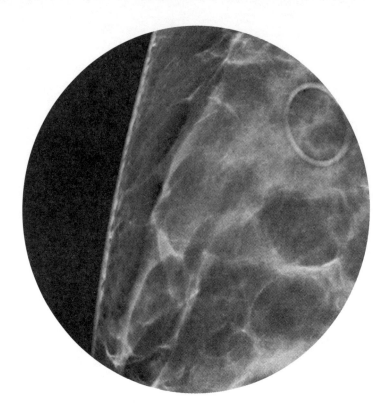

of femininity. Indeed of beauty. Of humanity itself. She has made it a thing not even living.

I should say that I like my doctor. I like her intellect and her manner. I like that she came endorsed by a friend I respect very much. I like that she isn't the doctor in my teens who wouldn't listen to me, openly skeptical of a teenage girl not having sex. I like that she isn't the doctor in my twenties who wouldn't talk to me, reserved any education on birth control for patients already in a committed relationship. I like that something about the salt-and-pepper streaks of her hair, the swing of it, never fails to remind me of my very dear friend Lee.

She could have said it was a bag of frozen peas. Or a bowl of corn kernels cleaved from the cob. She might have said it was a coin purse, a candy dish, a collection of baby teeth cupped in the palm, all the gumballs you could stuff into your cheeks on

a dare, a vase full of marbles sunk to settle the stems of a floral arrangement. But she didn't. These are not the clumps of bath salts before they fizz away. This is not marshmallows suspended in a Jell-O mold, the raisins lumping oatmeal, a muddy puddle choked with tadpoles. This is no champagne bucket full of ice cubes. This is no constellation waiting to be named.

* * * * * * * *

MY FRIEND JILL USED TO WALK THE DOG OF A WEALTHY FAM-ily by the lake. One summer they installed a new sculpture, and in excavating the earth to anchor it, had kicked up an old layer of white gravel that now mixed in with the slate gray. For a whole day they employed Jill to pick the white gravel out of the drive.

The pieces of gravel were so tiny, Jill said, and so profuse. It always seemed like you were close to finishing, that there couldn't possibly be more, that you almost had it, that they just couldn't have spread out and mixed in so inextricably. I imagine it like trying to recall all the lost grains of a saltshaker upended, a few tossed over the shoulder for good luck. One day didn't do it, and so she toiled for a week like this, plucking out the offending gravel. If it weren't for the pails she filled, she would not have known, would have had nothing to point to, that it made any difference at all.

· · · · · · · · ·

DALÍ OBSERVES, IN "POEM OF THE SMALL THINGS," ONE OF MY *girlfriend's breasts is a calm sea urchin, the other a swarming wasp's nest.*

· · · · · · · · ·

AFTER A LONG TIME, I DECIDE POMEGRANATE WOULD BE BET-ter: a thing that is a handful of seeds, that suggests the mingling of spring and the underworld. A red that stains your hands. A thing that splits open, bares itself to the sun and the rain and the piercing beak of a bird.

But the more I think of the sack of gravel, the more I love it. I am, in fact, thankful to have it. I start to know this even before I shrug the hospital gown back on at the exam, before I slip it off entirely to dress in my own clothes. I am given something broken but no longer breaking. It is as if the breast is gone, replaced with something useful. Considered and swapped out, like Indiana Jones in the temple, weighing sand and gold.

I had not been looking for alteration, but the barter made, I see that I have come out ahead: I have been traded something humble, plain even—but not vulnerable. I don't mind at all trading in some sign of femininity for unadulterated grit. It feels downright Amazonian. I don't mind all these lumps rendered inert, inorganic, known. It feels safer these days to be less female. I'm pleased. The gravel will do.

· · · · · · · · · · ·

WHAT WE KNOW ABOUT FREYDÍS EIRÍKSDÓTTIR, DAUGHTER of Eirík the Red and half sister of Leif Eiríksson, we know from the Vinland sagas, from two different accounts of the one story that is the reason we know her at all. We know her party is under attack; the warriors are fleeing—perhaps the shock of adversaries with catapults too much for the Vikings to comprehend. We know she has no sword until she takes one from a dead man, that she cannot run as fast as her warriors in retreat because she is very pregnant, that this slows her down, if she even tries to get away.

At the point of her capture, still shouting curses, admonishing her men who have fled in the face of attack, she is surrounded. Whatever threat she feels, whatever dread she knows, whatever canny or rage or madness floods her then, this woman encircled by the warriors of another people does not surrender to them. She pulls down her garment to expose one breast, brings her sword against it, and threatens to cut it off.

It is an act so shocking, so discomfiting, so utterly alien that all the standards of attack and capture, all the rules of violent conflict, are suspended. They leave her. *They* retreat.

· · · · · · · · · · ·

THE TECHNICIAN WHO ADMINISTERS THE NEXT MAMMOGRAM tells me there's no point in crying. Either there's nothing to worry about or crying won't help. I don't tell her about the gravel. I don't tell her about Freydís. I don't tell her about the worker from the Census Bureau who calls every six months with the same survey, gathering crime statistics this way because so many crimes are

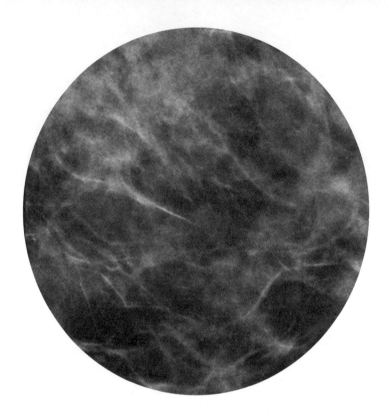

underreported. Sometimes on those phone calls we talk about my new job at the bookstore—the census worker and her sister are big readers—but always the census worker reads to me from the same script, asks every time about crime at the workplace and at school and at home, points out that we don't always think of it as crime when it's committed by a family member, acknowledges that sexual assault is difficult to talk about and then asks about that. She pins out a taxonomy of loss and pain in a chain of checkboxes we must tick off. It feels like beads on a rosary, the litany of "no" I give to her questions, a series of specters in the shadows, a string of blessings I should count.

I try to tell the mammogram technician she need not appeal to my reason. I try to tell her this sobbing is not a rational response. I try to tell her that this is the body doing it, that I can no more tell her why it is weeping than I can stop.

• • • • • • • • • • • •

DOWN THE HALL, WITH THE NEXT TECHNICIAN, I MAKE another image. No one shows me the mammograms, but in the sonogram, my breast looks like a moon. It is luminous. A perfect circle. Full and gray and pocked with a complicated landscape of rings and loops, as if my body were celestial and there had never been an atmosphere to blunt its history of meteor impacts, recorded in overlay, like a palimpsest.

The seas of the moon have wonderful names. Sea of Serpents, Sea of Showers; Sea of Nectar, Sea of Clouds. Of Vapors. Of Crises. Of Serenity. Mare Ingenii: Sea of Cleverness. Mare Marginis: Sea of the Edge. What else can one hope to think of after hearing it named, Mare Cognitum: *The Sea That Is Known*?

The sonogram technician does not say much. She is focused on her instruments. In the silence I am trying to string together the words to ask if I can have a picture of the sonogram. I am trying to decide if there is a way I can ask that will persuade her to stray from the routine. I think it must matter what words I use.

I have not found the right words to give the technician when she says what little she is going to. She points to the screen, and she calls these masses "islands." I find the word so beautiful. How beautiful to think: my breast a sea. I grew up with an ocean. It left specks of tar dotting the lining fabric of my swimsuits. It had jetties and pier pilings where I could marvel at how steadfast little barnacles push out the flat plane of their foundation into a curve, a caldera. How romantic to have an ocean in my breast, floating an archipelago. Sea of Islands. Ocean of Storms.

I want this word more even than the image I was trying to ask for. But when I ask her to confirm I heard it right, that *islands* is the word, she sounds defensive, seems to regret it, seems to want to take it back. She does not clarify whether she means the image or the flesh when she answers, answers as if there can be no arguing about it, as if I should drop it, as if by repeating what she has said I have endangered us both. "That's what they're called," she says. And in the gulf that follows, she spares me not another word.

10

MEGALONYX JEFFERSONII

I KNOW. YOU WANT TO TALK ABOUT THE GIANT SLOTH. YOU want to know why this particular giant sloth in this particular museum is wearing a hula skirt. That's fine. We'll get to that. But it will be easier if we start with the right terms. If you don't mind, then, first a few words on gender identity and the giant ground sloth, this giant ground sloth. Then we'll proceed.

By convention, Rusty is a him. Visitors encountering Rusty for the first time use the masculine pronoun instinctively, without even meaning to sex the sloth. I'm not reprimanding. Staff often make the same mistake. I myself still slip into saying "him," and I know better. I suspect that "him" happens because Rusty has so much character. Did you notice, for instance, his tongue wrapping around the reproduction oak leaves? His little tail curled in a half wag on the facsimile prairie floor? Anyway, my hunch is that we take a liking to the sloth and that inspires a kind of friendly familiarity, which leads to the possibly benign if thoroughly unscientific personification of him. It's all very natural to say "him." But it's wrong.

Rusty is a model. A fiberglass form covered over with wiry hair clipped from thousands of modern-day cows' tails. The bristly faux fur was all dyed to the same muddy red—browsers tend to be monochromatic, after all—the hue itself suggested by the auburn fur of a related sloth find excavated in South America. You're right: South America is a long way from Iowa. It was a little closer in the Late Pleistocene. But no, not a lot closer.

I was saying: Rusty is a model. An object. Hence, sexless; ergo an it. It has no visible mammary glands, no sex organs of any kind. Its eyelashes have mostly broken off. Even if the model makers had been less prudish, had possessed enough information to fashion detectable primary or secondary sex characteristics, those features still wouldn't be particularly meaningful, not in the way of the specimen skins: the fading foxes and cracking zebras and hundred-year-old sparrows postured throughout Mammal Hall and the Hageboeck Hall of Birds upstairs. And this difference in the origins of models and specimens, the difference between what never was and what no longer is, is why we can dress up Rusty. Models are governed by a different code of ethics than specimens. We wouldn't put so much as a paper crown on a specimen.

A lot of people fail to notice that Rusty is not, in fact, a specimen. I understand. It's a dark room. The wall text is unobtrusive and dimly lit. The informational paragraph is intentionally kept brief enough that you'll bother to read through to the part about this being an extinct species from the Ice Age, but it's posted at adult eye level, and children rush beneath it, crowd along the guardrail and call out to their parents and guides and chaperones to see what they see, to bear witness to this enormous and unbelievable creature parked on its haunches and forever drawing down a leafy branch with four eight-inch claws. It could distract you from ever reading anything.

And clearly extinction alone is not enough to rule out Rusty being a specimen. We have specimens of extinct species on view throughout the museum. None quite so old as *Megalonyx jeffersonii*, perhaps, but natural history is nothing if not a sequence of unlikely and unexpected events—that we are standing here upright with the language to have this conversation perhaps the most unlikely one of all. If you believe in the feathered reptiles and the egg-laying mammals and the fossil ferns and the Devonian ocean, why shouldn't we have the original hide of a ten-thousand-year-old ground sloth taxidermied and on display? Isn't that exactly what we would do if we had one? How could you be expected to know that Rusty is only speculation, the painstaking and flawed interpretation of a thing we know only from fragment?

The first thing Rusty ever wore was a tie. Two ties, actually, purchased one at a time from the university bookstore across the street, the second tie after it became very apparent that the first would scarcely encircle the giant sloth's throat. David Brenzel refers to this observation as Sloth Dressing Lesson #1: Scale.

Dr. Brenzel pioneered sloth dressing. In 1999, the faculty senate was scheduled to hold a reception in the University of Iowa Museum of Natural History's galleries. The president of the faculty senate, looking around, asked the director of the museum, George Schrimper, if something could be done to "make the place less stuffy." Shortly thereafter, against Dr. Schrimper's better judgment, Dr. Brenzel's curatorial authority expanded to include spiffing up the sloth. You can imagine: a necktie-wearing sloth the size of a small elephant was rather droll and very well received by the assorted academics and administrators milling through Iowa Hall with drinks in their hands. Dr. Schrimper said nothing. Dr. Brenzel started thinking about Halloween.

Halloween is the core of sloth dressing. It's the only consistently recognized holiday on the sloth calendar, and every year Rusty wears something new. The first costume, the one that founded this tradition, was Zorro. Specifically, the 1981 George Hamilton *Zorro, the Gay Blade* Zorro, with black eye mask and teeth-clenched rose and ball-fringed Spanish gaucho hat and everything.

With the exception of Halloween, the official sloth calendar remains in flux, observing a motley and intermittent combination of holidays and cultural events. You may see Rusty with wings and bow and heart-tipped arrows on Valentine's Day. It's a top hat and dark beard for Lincoln's Birthday—or a white beard and HMS *Beagle* seasickness bag on Darwin Day. Then there's Pilgrim sloth. Olympic athlete. Santa. Rudolph. King Tut, complete with pipe-cleaner eyeliner. Curiously, Rusty has yet to honor Thomas Jefferson, though the former president's 1797 paper on *Megalonyx* is arguably the founding American publication in vertebrate paleontology, and it's the man himself honored by a French scientist in the species name, *jeffersonii*. Perhaps we'll get to that next year. We've been busy. Sure, the butterfly net was on hand, but it takes a while to find a pith helmet big enough for explorer sloth. I think we all know leprechaun costumes don't make themselves.

Rusty was always meant to catch your attention, to be what they called an "Oh, wow!" moment when the museum was redesigned in 1984. At the time there were plenty of mammoths and mastodons in other museums; so this museum (the second-oldest museum west of the Mississippi River) commissioned the first life-size model of an Ice Age sloth and strategically stationed it here near the south entrance where any of three main paths will deliver you. It may be the most important exhibition decision here since the 1914 unveiling of Dr. Homer Dill's cyclorama of Laysan Island revolutionized, no circular pun intended, the art of dioramic presentation.

When we first met, Rusty was sporting white bunny ears and a powder-puff tail, a larger-than-life carrot dangling from the half-open maw where usually there's a mouthful of leaves. Outside, the wind was chill and biting and March. Inside, there was Easter sloth. It was all very incongruous. And marvelous. And right. It was precisely the moment when I realized that Iowa and I would get along just fine, that this was perhaps the very sort of place I would have been searching for, if I'd had any idea it could exist.

And that was months before Sarah Horgen granted me sloth-dressing privileges. Before I moved here and she let me design new costumes and suggest new holidays the sloth might observe. It was certainly before I knew that to reach around Rusty's neck, to drape a toga or adjust a cape or straighten a collar, my cheek would have to brush the sloth's and the fingertips of my left hand would only just touch the fingertips of my right.

Ms. Horgen, the museum's education and outreach coordinator, was thinking about Sloth Dressing Lesson #1 at the fabric store in October as she charged to a museum account five yards of red felt and a slightly smaller amount of red silk lining. The clerk ringing her up asked in a chummy kind of way if she was working on a Halloween costume.

"Little Red Riding Hood," Ms. Horgen replied. Ms. Horgen wavers on whether it's worth going into detail while on these errands.

The clerk squinted. "That's a big trick-or-treater," she said.

Little Red Riding Hood had not been Ms. Horgen's first choice. Ms. Horgen had been hoping for Marilyn Monroe, but for logistical reasons was suggesting maybe a vampire or mad scientist or some such thing when she entrusted me with designing and constructing Rusty's costume that year. Ms. Horgen is one of the people who doesn't say "him" when she talks about Rusty. Nor does she say "it." Ms. Horgen is part of a growing contingent that says "her."

Rusty, as I have explained, is, emphatically, an it. But the specimen Rusty is based on, the American Falls discovery, well, that's another story. Rusty is intended to represent Iowa's Ice Age megafauna, but it's the rare Iowa sloth that's found even thirty bones complete, which leaves a lot to be inferred. So, because a sloth skull collected in Turin, Iowa, is almost identical to one found at American Falls, Idaho, Rusty's proportions are borrowed from the more complete specimen. *More* complete is an understatement. The American Falls discovery is the *most* complete giant sloth specimen ever found: not a bone missing from the waist up.

It's what's missing from the waist down, however, that leaves Rusty's gender identification up for debate. That debate got a lot livelier when H. Gregory McDonald suggested in a 2005 paper that, based on comparative analysis of the diastema of the jaw, the American Falls specimen was, in fact, female.

It's gotten a bit heated. Holmes Semken, leader of the Tarkio Valley Sloth Project, discounts the available sample set as inadequate to prove that the smaller specimens are the females—the reverse is certainly true for some mammals. Dr. Brenzel stresses that it may not be sexual dimorphism at all, but merely individual variation. Both Dr. Semken and Dr. Brenzel are at pains to underscore that a mistake is entirely possible in the McDonald conjecture. Heck, the smaller specimens could be juveniles! There's just not enough information to reach a consensus. Which, conversely, also means there's not enough data to discount this surprisingly inflammatory thesis: Rusty was a girl.

You'd never guess it from the costumes. Not until recently, anyway. In the last six months Rusty has evoked Little Red Riding Hood, the Statue of Liberty, and Rosie the Riveter— in honor of Halloween, Election Day, and Women's History Month, respectively. But before that, in a decade of sloth dressing and some twenty-two documented costumes, there was maybe one even arguably hinting at a female icon or traditionally feminine attire or anything not obviously masculine or patently ambiguous. Yes, exactly. The hula sloth.

You wanted to know about the hula skirt, why Rusty is wearing one? Why indeed. Because the Hawaii-based animated film *Lilo and Stitch* opened in 2002 and Rusty has a thing for movie premieres. Because outside it is warm after so long being frozen. Because I asked for the ring of small brass keys and opened every storage panel in Iowa Hall until I found the grass skirts and the leis knotted together and long enough to span, respectively, a twelve-foot waist and a fifty-inch neck. The efficient cause, the final cause, it's all the same thing. We dress the sloth because it amuses us. Because it's strangely compelling. Because we are drawn to it for what it is, even as we want to make it something else. Because, how else to say this, it needs to be done.

Dr. Schrimper was always a little worried about Rusty, you know. George was a stickler for proper procedure and best practice, and he sensed the power of Rusty to eclipse everything else he loved about the museum. It doesn't, I don't think, but he worried. True: a big thing can obstruct the big picture. One can introduce a single element and have it overwhelm or belittle or change everything else. He didn't want this to be a museum of the sloth—he said that a lot. But he never said anything about his staff dressing up Rusty. He understood, I think. He didn't need to ask why.

11

THE GHOST OF CHRISTMAS ALWAYS

*I have endeavored in this Ghostly little book,
to raise the Ghost of an Idea. . . .
May it haunt their houses pleasantly.*

—CHARLES DICKENS

THERE IS NO DOUBT THAT SCROOGE WAS HIRED. THIS MUST BE distinctly understood, or nothing wonderful can come of the story I am going to relate.

The way I heard it was from a mezzo-soprano. The mezzo-soprano heard it from a Buddhist tenor, between choruses of "God Rest Ye Merry Gentlemen," in the gaps between arriving guests, heard the story clad in velvet voice when they were not called to serve in complicated four-part harmonies.

There is always conversation, always stories, always talk. The minute guests are out of earshot, the carolers do not sing a note. Which may seem miserly, but the voice is a resource. You could be hired to sing every day in December, if you wanted, though you are not paid to sing, exactly—you are paid to be heard. You are paid to shape your body so that it makes a sound that will reach another body you will not otherwise touch. You do it because of what it is to tune a chord, to make one out of many, but you are paid to be part of the decorations. You are paid for your ability to create and release tension. You are paid to return once more to all this music you've sung since you started singing—not just the carols everyone knows, but the obscure ones, the Burgundian ancient ones, the ones old enough to be dark at the edges, like tarnish, though that is why they shine.

The quartet was also hired. Like the caterers in the kitchen. Like the fortune teller off in the study, aswirl in red and green plaids. Like Rudolph squeaking past you in the mansion stairwell, that corridor maze where you are tucked away out of view for a few minutes, hoop skirt collapsed against the wall, to take your contract-stipulated break.

The mezzo-soprano and the tenor have been singing together in the quartet for fifteen years, and the tenor and the bass have sung together longer than that. They have all been known to interject words into the lyrics to make a bawdy variation. The quartet knows all the inappropriate word substitutions and stresses in the caroling book. They know the way no one but their conspirators hears the aberration if only one of them does it. And they know the professional straight face of recovery, a cover of its own, should, every so often, entirely by chance, all of them voice it at once.

All this time, all these intimacies, and they aren't sure they'd recognize one another in their street clothes. They know it must be otherwise, but they picture one another in their costumes: running errands or making dinner or going to the gym in fur muffs and hats trimmed with holly. However likely another version, however true it must be, it's hard to imagine the other in the attire of normal life. It can be hard to believe a thing you haven't seen. Though I will admit that sometimes, the thing you've only heard about sounds truer than the words you know by heart.

They say this Scrooge looks thoroughly, inside out, like Scrooge. He has real muttonchops. He has a waistcoat and a cravat and a silk hat. He has breeches and those shoes with conspicuous buckles. His prescription is set in olde-tyme spectacles pinched at the end of his nose. His body is all rusty wire spring, tense and brittle, prone in equal measure to lurch or hunch.

They say he's very amiable, all things told, but when he's on the clock, he will start lurking. He'll drop comments about the outfits, the party, the food. Miserly comments. Gruff. He doesn't so much bah or humbug. He fingers the drapes or squints at the sherry, inspects the cloth of your lapel and spits out, "This cost a pretty penny, what?!"

And the guests *love* it. It is the highlight of the night. Scrooge is the crowning glory, the finishing touch, the sour cherry on top of the most exclusive invite in town—the luxury and the opulence and the excess not enough until there is someone to point it out and disparage it, the way the best perfumes aren't perfect without a note of rot.

Scrooge is hired to tell the well-to-do they are wasting their money, and they can't get enough. How merry! How droll! It *is* too much, isn't it? Happy Christmas! How entirely, essentially, deliciously just like us: we pay to have the truth confirmed and then to laugh it off. We crave both. We cannot get enough. We want to be known *and* to be forgiven, to be caught and then set free.

Oh! but he was a tight-fisted hand at the grindstone, Scrooge! A squeezing, wrenching, grasping, scraping, clutching, covetous old sinner!

Parsimony derives from the Latin *parsimonia*, meaning frugality and thrift, only later acquires the connotation of stinginess, becomes a synonym for Scrooge. *Dickens*, on the other hand, might as well be a synonym for abundance. The English-speaking world may have canonized only *A Christmas Carol*, but he wrote quite a few Christmas novellas, plus dozens more Christmas stories, and when he could write no more recruited contributors to help fill out whole Christmas issues of his two-penny journal *Household Words*. He published *A Christmas Carol* insisting on the extra loveliness of color illustrations, lavish, and was almost undone by the cost.

He writes, absolutely understandably, very much like someone compensated by the word. Even Dickensian titling overflows, spilling inevitably into subtitle, always that shadow of a second line. The subtitles of the Christmas books include *A Goblin Story, A Love Story, A Ghost Story, A Fancy for Christmas-Time, A Fairy Tale of Home*. As if the Christmas spirit were a hermit crab, crawling through shell after shell. As if anything might be a vessel.

We could have pinned Christmas to his crickets or chemists or battlefields, to a man in disguise or a dog named Boxer. He offered them all, fable after fable for us to inhabit. In their day there was some competition for most popular, but ultimately, collectively, we fell for the ghost story. And now we refuse to let it go.

I love the story the mezzo-soprano says the tenor tells the quartet about rich folk employing a kind of cranky Cassandra, how it points to something true. But if I like it for how it opens, I adore it all the more for how it ends, for the coda, the kicker, the part told if there's time enough on break in the mansion stairwell between bites of figgy pudding the caterer could spare, enough time between arrivals in the tent on the front walk next to the silver urn of hot chocolate.

It's not simply that Scrooge was hired as critic, as sourpuss, as professional gadfly—and that this was the darling cherished moment of the toniest fete in the Metroplex—it's that, they say, one year he wasn't hired, and he came anyway. They say he keeps coming, and he hasn't been paid for years.

I love to think there was such joy in being misanthropic that it was worth doing for free. It makes sense that, having learned how to bend the ear of the elite, you might keep speaking truth to power, as a matter of principle, for as long as you possibly could. All sorts of things, once summoned, are difficult to dismiss. But I have my own pet theory about how these things happen. I suspect there's something more.

"This is the only story of mine whose moral I know," Kurt Vonnegut wrote in the novel *Mother Night*. "We are what we pretend to be, so we must be careful about what we pretend to be."

If you spent enough time in the guise of Scrooge, inhabiting him, all those days breathing Scrooge in and out, some of it might stick. Don't actors talk about this phenomenon? Of taking it home? Of breaking down hours later in the middle of an interview because you'd come from a scene where you had to bury your son? I mean, if you channeled someone long enough, you might be transformed too.

And hard to say: if you inhabited Ebenezer, you might be transformed into the heartless spoilsport we meet in the first pages—or you, too, might be saved. Who is Scrooge in the last pages of *A Christmas Carol* but someone glad to give freely? Where do we find him but at a party that once asked him to come, yet which he was not expected to attend?

Scrooge has become a shorthand for *grinch*, for cold unfeeling spite, but it's worth noting that's not the point of the story. We pin him to the Scrooge we meet in the opening scenes, keep him bitter and withholding even though his arc is wholly a matter of changing his ways. As if we stopped reading a few chapters in, as if we left at intermission, as if we did not believe in change, we seem studiously to ignore the after in the diptych of Scrooge. I wager no one has ever said *Scrooge* and meant a person who's undergone radical rehabilitation, who saw the light, who turned it around *just in time* and became the very model of repentance and generosity and charity and mirth. We love the version that is unlovable; what to do with this other guy?

"He kept coming even after they stopped hiring him," the mezzo-soprano says about Scrooge. "I don't know if that's true at all. But every year we mention it."

. . . tumbling out into the street in their apoplectic opulence . . .

Statisticians, too, believe in parsimony. The world is so wildly, impossibly complex. You would think that elaboration would get ever closer to evoking that, honestly portraying it, that any semblance of accuracy would demand every species of detail and caveat and footnote and special case, that we would descend into fractal eddies of addendum and embellishment with a close enough look at anything—but we don't. We are Zeno, ever approaching but unable to close the gap. And how close do we really want to come? Note the special propensity of clones and doppelgängers and anything not quite across the uncanny valley to creep us out. Better to quit while we're ahead, really. Less is more. The representation is always some degree of approximation, and the best we can do is hem it in.

The insight "all models are wrong" is an old one. It is an idea found in various language across time and place and discipline, but these days the specific aphorism is generally attributed to the statistician George Box, who used it more than once in a 1976 paper and most perfectly, most crystalline memorably, in the construction, "All models are wrong, but some are useful."

It all but proves itself, really, the way this particular insight is squared away and given attribution, seems to *need* it, is such provocative common sense that we yearn for a way to say it succinctly, pin it to a source and cite it with authority, draw this thing out of the ether and into a definable body. The very notion that it sprang uniquely from any one particular individual is clearly wrong and yet, still, so very useful.

The writer Nathan Heller observed that there are two kinds of ideas: sunflowers and bougainvillea. Sunflowers are clear and singular and robust. You know exactly when you have one. Such an idea isolates beautifully. It makes for a good TED talk. But it is not more real or more accurate or more right for being easier to grasp.

There are also ideas like bougainvillea, those sprays of papery white or orange or fuchsia bracts, bright as petals and veined liked leaves. The bougainvillea, on every level, resists being any one thing. It is frost-sensitive *and* hardy, ornamental *and* thorny, naturally prone to hybrids, and many cultivars double-flowered and variegated. It is possible the first European to observe one was the French botanist Jeanne Baret, the first woman to circumnavigate the globe, a feat possible in 1769 only because she passed as a man—the botanist, too, two things at once, an image and a body.

Bougainvillea ideas are all constellation and accumulation. Maybe not complicated but complex, containing multitudes. Pluck a single stem and it wilts as if melted, cannot be sustained as solitary exemplar, is not a thing like that.

If you thought the bougainvillea was just its tiny, simple, waxy white flower, you would miss almost everything. But how to hold this fraction of the four o'clock family, this genus that is tree and bush and vine? What do we do with things that cannot be distilled?

You might think the statisticians would just leave it at that—parsimony—if only for the sheer we're-done-here mic drop elegance of it. But even this most minimalist of principles cannot resist expansion.

"Since all models are wrong the scientist must be alert to what is importantly wrong," Box continues. Some inaccuracies are the very liberties that serve to clarify and illuminate in the first place, so we needn't boycott maps and diagrams and schemas out of hand, we can probably hold on to our parables and fables and myths, but we should aspire to "worrying selectively." We must remain vigilant, but only on the lookout for those species of infidelity that taint or distort or obscure. As Box also wrote, though it is quoted far less often, "It is inappropriate to be concerned about mice when there are tigers abroad."

Selectively, then, we needn't worry that actual mice directly transmit hantavirus and hemorrhagic fever and a dozen other diseases, indirectly contribute to a dozen more. Nor should we lose any sleep over the fact that mice are vastly more numerous and close at hand. We hardly need telling: a metaphor is a model too.

You may be an undigested bit of beef, a blot of mustard, a crumb of cheese, a fragment of an underdone potato. There's more of gravy than of grave about you, whatever you are!

The common house mouse, *Mus musculus*, is what's known as a model organism. Tigers aren't, but more than a hundred other species are, among them *E. coli* and baker's yeast and watercress and zebra fish and fruit flies and soybeans and nematodes and rats and rice and the slime mold *Dictyostelium discoideum*. However much it sounds like an award for citizenship or attendance, *model organism* is a technical term for those strains of species cultivated to be as close to standard, reliable, interchangeably and unchangingly equal as a living thing can be.

The selection of these species has to do with science looking at the great wide world and taking a special interest in the workings of two categories: what humans eat, and what can stand in for some aspect of our own biology. Basically, these are our twin priorities: what nourishes our bodies and what echoes their decay. We elevate for study that which would sustain us. And we will, one way or another, consume the bodies of others for some chance of making sense of our own.

The first mammal domesticated for research was a rat. *Rattus norvegicus*, to be precise, the brown rat or city rat or wharf rat or water rat or sewer rat or common rat or Norway rat, though it most likely originates from Asia. Its virtues as a model organism are both that it models the human immune system and that we otherwise do not wish to see ourselves as rats. The recognition and the disavowal are both crucial. The rat must be like us and yet not a thing we think is like us or we would not cultivate it as a stand-in.

Rat domestication goes back to seventeenth-century Japan, with the selective breeding of European and North American laboratory populations a product of the nineteenth century—one more Victorian enthusiasm we cannot seem to shake.

For ages, Western biology looked out and out and out, running nets across the fields and sailing expeditions across the globe and trying by sheer capture to get a handle on what all there is that's living, breathing, dying here. It is a methodology of expansion, of excess, the articulating of every last detail, life a cup that runneth over. Then the rise of model organisms signals a kind of contraction, a single-mindedness, a parsimony, a retreat back to what is finite and controlled.

The world is wild, run amok, but in our lab organisms we promote an unnatural homogeneity, prize their stability, the way they don't as a population particularly change over time, and not at all, if we can help it. The ultimate creature not stirring, if you will.

There is a kind of knowing that is possible by stasis, by stopping, by fixing in ether or pinning to a board or breeding as if to make a clone. How else to tamp down the onslaught of variables in this moveable feast of a world?

And yet, of course, to arrest on this dynamic planet is a change of its own. We've noted for at least a century the distinctions between lab rats and their wild relatives, how quickly they diverged, the way we have made them not a model of ratness but something else, eternal, out of time and in the image of ourselves.

I daresay, we've made ghosts of less.

> *. . . which, being only light, was more alarming than a dozen ghosts, as he was powerless to make out what it meant, or would be at; and was sometimes apprehensive that he might be at that very moment an interesting case of spontaneous combustion, without having the consolation of knowing it.*

"At Rent Santa DFW, we have a performer who special-
izes in the character of Ebenezer Scrooge." And "At Fun Time
Entertainment, we have an actor who can come to your party
as Scrooge and entertain your guests!" And "Do you have questions about Scrooge? We would love to talk with you about
him! Just give us a call. . ."

These three postings still haunt the internet, are unstuck in
time and live on. So if you do, in fact, have questions about
Scrooge, if you follow the instructions from the past and ring
up the booker in the present, she'll have to be the one to break it
to you: "There's not a great Scrooge to hire in Dallas."

Oh, she knows exactly whom you've called about—"He was
wonderful. He was so *good* at that character. He did it for years."
Even among the balloon artist elves and the real-beard Santas, he
stood out. But there was only ever the one him, and you can't hire
him anymore, and no one else has filled his block-heeled shoes.

It's important that you stay on the line, though. Drift into
your future. Wait a beat in your disappointment, in the predictable confirmation that we can't have nice things and nothing
gold can stay and of course you can't summon a fiction or the
past. Hold there, in this being more or less what you expected,
the world all dead ends and dry creeks. Stay there, silent, right
up until she says one more thing and instead of contracting, the
world bursts open, your eyes wide as you trip down the rabbit
hole into a warren of echo and shadow and what shouldn't be
but is nonetheless humming away and here we are.

Because if you aren't looking to book anyone anyway ("You
just have questions, right?"), and if you'll give her a minute to
text her girlfriend ("What was his *name*?!"), and if you dare to
risk the story you cherish just to chase whatever scrap of truth
may once in some version have seeded it—well, there's another
number you can ring.

"That's a wonderful story," Bo Gerard says to me when I explain why I'm calling, tell him the story I've heard. "And like most wonderful stories, it simply isn't true."

I have called to get the story from Scrooge himself, and he is emphatic—really rather on brand, actually—tells me almost first thing, like a mantra, like sage advice, like common sense: "Never give away the only thing you have to sell."

For forty-one years—by his calculations some fourteen thousand performances—Bo Gerard was hired out as a comedy magician, almost always under his own name. Before he was the model Scrooge at the apex of Dallas Christmas, Bo Gerard trained in theater and European clowning. In the latter tradition, the idea is to discover who you really are and embellish *that*. Your faults are bigger, your strengths are bigger, but the very essence of it is: you can't get lost in a persona until you find yourself first.

Only then, and only occasionally, if the party was appropriately themed, did he do the same close-up magic act but in another character. There were different characters for different parties, a handful of iterations and experiments, but ultimately only two alter egos ever stuck.

"I did Groucho as well, at Hollywood parties. And I could say things at a party as Groucho I could never say as me." Wagging a cigar and propositioning a matron in furs was not unlike being Ebenezer at the Christmas tree lighting in Plano, where, in a parade of performers waving and smiling, he could be the only one to stick his tongue out and blow raspberries. "There's an allowance given to these characters, the jesters and Kokopelli—as long as you play them all the way through."

He didn't lose himself in Scrooge. He was never a baddie pro bono. Peak Scrooge was 1990–2005, and he hasn't been Scrooge at all for a decade or more. But he stopped, he says, because it was such a difficult character. Technically Dallas *can* produce a white Christmas, but it's more likely to be eighty degrees and there you are with all those layers of clothing, plus a wig and a hat, trying to be festive and engaging. You could get over that part, of course. There's a lot you can carry. But there was no way to recover when the audience itself changed.

"I did a lot of corporate work back when people wanted to turn their chairs around in a ballroom and pay attention," Bo says. "Twenty-five years ago, no one was asking, 'Why is this guy coming to my table?'"

He's married to a performer and she noticed it too, how the lines for balloon animals were long and happy when the wait was for a fun exchange and the shock of a request made real, but grew short and curt and restless as patrons came to believe, impatient with every breath, that they were there for a balloon. COVID lockdowns and precautions put the coffin nail in close-up magic, but he'd all but stopped doing interactive entertainment a decade before the pandemic.

Bo figures that people increasingly on devices were less used to reacting out loud, less used to interacting with live entertainment, less used to being with one another in the first place. Meanwhile, nationally televised shows asked even home audiences to be judges, and everything we bought or ate or consumed could be rated and reviewed. It might seem passive on its face, but there's an art to being an audience. It cultivates a certain kind of suspension, a generosity, a hope. It asks a mass of people to collectively take a certain kind of risk, to be game, ready both to amplify and to absorb.

Event planners still called, of course, eager to book Bo's act, but then they would hedge: "The only thing is, the client doesn't want any interaction."

The magic was never the substance of the act. Bo says, "Magic was simply a way to break into a crowd, make them into an audience." It was always a conduit, a connection, an avenue to give and take, the thing you could see that allowed you to tap into something you couldn't otherwise access.

That's what the audience appreciated, not the showmanship or the skill or the sleight of hand, but to be transformed into their open, believing, astonished selves. Great big ballrooms or groups of four people, didn't matter, it took no time to unite them, delight them, have them in the palm of your hand. "That's the gig: break in, take control, then release it." Then you find out what they really want.

But the wisdom of our ancestors is in the simile; and my unhallowed hands shall not disturb it, or the Country's done for.

There are reindeer grazing on the lawn. The mansion landscaping is decidedly not the tundra, or the subarctic or boreal climes they come from, but neither are they drawing sleds or yielding their bodies as milk or meat or hide, so maybe they don't mind the Bermuda grass.

Most of the five hundred some species of holly are from the tropics and subtropics, are represented in Europe by only a single species bright against the snow—*Ilex aquifolium,* both the type species and the poster child of holiday décor—but somehow half the Christmas-observing world says "holly" and means only one thing.

Up in the suburbs, Prestonwood Baptist Church promises "flying angels, live animals, the Living Nativity and much more!" Should you want to be there, if you want to *see* the camels, the burros and sheep, maybe a zebra and some peacocks and a choir one thousand strong and who knows what else, you have to be sitting at your computer ready to pounce when tickets go on sale, stalk them in the virtual marketplace before they're sold out faster than the Rolling Stones. Frankly, you'd be more likely to find room at the inn.

Maybe all Christmas is wrong, but some is useful. If this is a holiday centered on the ultimate ineffable and the emphatically corporeal—*the Lord God made flesh*—I sometimes wonder, How is that not enough? How can that fail to stand still? How can it resemble a story that no longer inhabits an audience, grasping but unable to make us one?

But I can see why we shroud even this story in Dickens. We spend our lives making sense of the material through the immaterial and back again. We know when to welcome a stand-in or a proxy. We fixate or isolate or make the one instance iconic. We have our strategies. And we leave behind our chatter, our talk, scatter our stories beyond our bodies and within them.

I can see why the quartet always cycles back to the story of Scrooge unbidden. The ghost of an idea is like that. I, too, am fed by the vision of someone at the top of their game, unconstrained by contract or expectation but electric in their genius, a body utterly alive, moving through the world not alone but on their own terms and by their own light. I have no model for what doesn't either collapse back to the source or splinter off until some fragment, some variation on the theme, takes on a life of its own.

It's now a story I tell. And maybe, like most stories, it is about the ideas that haunt us, the individual a stand-in for something more, a body changed by forces we mostly cannot see, and always—ever—the reverberation of ghost after ghost. All of it expanding and contracting, fluid then fixed, invoked and dispelled and invoked again. I mean, what miracle is not about the body? What happens if we don't become what we pretend? Why do we ever hold our breath—and under whose power do we let it go?

THE HALF STORY

Above all was the sense of hearing acute. I heard all things in the heaven and in the earth. I heard many things in hell. How, then, am I mad? Hearken! and observe how healthily—how calmly I can tell you the whole story.

—EDGAR ALLAN POE

WE ARE SHAPED BY FORCES WE CANNOT SEE. OF COURSE WE are. Constantly. Almost by nothing else. We are calibrated to a certain window of wavelengths, of time, of space. We are limited to our frameworks. Everything else is too big. Or too small. Too far. Too near. Too fast. Too slow. Too indirect. Too overwhelmingly the ether or else too consumingly close. So much beyond our comprehension or else beneath us, buried, banished, or embedded within us. We are shaped by forces we cannot see. And still, we know they are there.

I smelled it first. That ancient olfactory sense, capable of such subtlety, of absolute nuance, instead assaulted by the raw dank pungency of it. A reek you hope is only something died in the wall. Rot a more polite association, putrid the lesser evil, a body in the transition of decay the most optimistic gloss of such fetid acid musk.

I remember a class I took on color photography: the plasticky paper, the chemistry so nasty it was quarantined inside big blocky machines, the work of exposure a matter of focusing light but otherwise the maze of the darkroom all but pitch-black. There was a grope to getting out, a tiny act of faith, a memory of the map and my place in it. Occasionally I got turned around and was not sure I would ever find my bearings. And then always, eventually, I got far enough in the right direction and the walls yielded. I pushed back a velvet curtain and the light was blinding.

The machine, working through a process of its own, then spat out my test strip, and I'd stick it with a magnet to the board and try to see how far off I was. The eye is so good. Or rather, the brain is so ready to adjust, so capable of translation and invention, that you have only a few seconds before you'll accommodate the ten points yellow or the five magenta and read the colors you think should be there. To stave it off there was a way you held up a filter of cellophane to look through, a fluttering flick of the frame there-there-there-gone, there-there-there-gone so you could hold a point of comparison, could see what was right before your eyes, could decide what to do next before the compensation hit, before you couldn't distinguish between what was there and how it should be.

The smell was not like that. It was adamant. Insistent. Impossible to get used to. Intolerable, perhaps, but who could stick around to find out? It was, in so many ways, concentrated—seemed confined to my childhood bedroom and present nowhere else in the house. I opened the windows that still worked and left the room.

→ → →

THE WINTER AFTER THAT SUMMER I WAS VISITING AGAIN, arrived first at my brother's place, having agreed to ferry my nieces with me to see their Nana and PopPop. I thought I should prepare them. My mother said the stench wasn't that bad now, barely noticeable, but it wasn't clear anyone could sleep in that room and the girls might be caught in the shuffle of habitable spaces, so I tried to explain.

There is a smell, I said. There is evidence there is a creature. Maybe there only *was* a creature, but I think it would be naive at this point to expect it has decamped or decomposed. You maybe haven't been close enough to a bird colony to understand, never walked under the bridges or branches suspending a whole colony of bats, but there is a certain accretion of excretion that is breathtaking. *Acrid* doesn't do it justice. Nor *rank*. Guano is a study in intensity, positively elemental, all that nitrogen and phosphate and potassium, all the chemicals good for growing plants and no small number of them good for making things explode, excrement mixed up with feather and bone and corpses, intimately off-putting, a threshold smell of both life and death.

What kind of creature? they wanted to know.

Bat guano shouldn't smell so much, I reasoned. We aren't so close to the coast that seabirds should have nested in the eaves. Doubtless it's not a harbor seal wedged into the ceiling upstairs. I don't know, I said. Let's call it Mortimer.

I have strong feelings about the made-up names I use, particularly in the world I offer to children. I don't want to imply there is a default of gender or geography or era. I want old-fashioned monikers and localized nicknames and allusions and puns to get their turns. If I'd been faster on my feet I would have called it Mrs. Rochester, and there might be no more story to tell. But one also has only so many moments to come up with a name when put on the spot, two beats to seize upon it, whatever it is, though much would later be read into "Mortimer." Like the first black-and-white draft of Mickey Mouse, a poet friend points out, raising an eyebrow of significance. Like a dead sea, my mother says ominously, holding a book of baby names, or else a dead pond.

We don't even know if it is an it, I tell the nieces. It might be a them.

Or a her, the nieces cheer from the back seat.

Quite possibly, yes, but I'm saying Mortimer may be a family. Or Mortimer may be two Mortimers fighting. Mortimer may be a series of roommates and sublessors and stand-ins and substitute teachers collectively amounting to Mortimer. This may be Mortimer I, II, III, and IV all together or in succession over time. This may be two friends in a Mortimer suit. This may be the Dread Pirate Roberts as Mortimer or Mortimer as the Dread Pirate Roberts. Mortimer may be a mother, making more and more and more Mortimerlings.

THIS TIME I HEARD IT. OR ELSE I HEARD THEM. CERTAINLY IT was not just one sound. The scraping, first. Then what sounded for all the world like the rhythmic, labored footfall of a full-grown human being. Eventually, a whole orchestra of concatenation. I came to know its rasping scratching shuffle, its thudding scramble brushwork, the precise focused industry of it, the grope and guess and fumble of it, the thump, the turn-around, the dig.

There was a certain scrim of terror to it all. I could not determine the structural stability overhead, the tensile strength of a substance possibly gnawed away. And so I lived with the possibility Mortimer might breach, bust in, crash through the ceiling and Kool-Aid Man into my life, wildness itself, all shock and claws and thrashing fury, the chalk of plaster dust as the ceiling gave way so palpable in this scenario I was surprised, when I looked, that the ceiling was, as it ever had been, composite beams and three-inch strips of cedar plank.

But for all my apprehension, all my hours lying on the bed facing a sky I could not see, it was easier to live with now that it was Mortimer. I could suspend my concern, relax my alarm long enough to be curious, to attend to it. I began to take note first of the percussion, then to ponder its source.

It's probably on the roof, my father says. My father dreamed this house, walked through every feature with the architect, but I don't know how long it's been since he's actually gone upstairs. It is 100 percent inside the roof, I tell him. Perhaps by now it is *of* the roof, *with* the roof, any number of prepositions, but not merely *on*. Mortimer is not a cat burglar or a chimney sweep. Mortimer is embedded. Mortimer may be above, but also certainly, no question, definitively within.

In the walls, it is the cask of amontillado. Under the floorboards, it is the tell-tale heart. But what do we entomb in the attic, save one portrait of a beautiful young man and all the women we have deemed mad? Sometimes Heidi or Pollyanna or the little princess, orphan girls come to live with a gruff but wounded grown-up? Is Rapunzel imprisoned in an attic? What else is ever in that in-between, not even attic but the liminal nameless gap that apparently exists between ceiling and roof?

"An attic is not a story." I read this as I try to understand at least the architecture, the fascia and soffit and scantlings of it all, and I feel so chastened, so suddenly called out for any latent impulse to impose a narrative that it takes a minute to read it just as a definition and not as a personal rebuke. Maybe an attic is not a story, but in a story it has its place, functions as a place of the mind, of secrets, of storage, of at the very least Jo March in her scribbling suit, black as ink stains, willing herself to be a writer, her pencils nibbled upon by rats.

I wonder about the illumination, if Mortimer sees or if it is a navigation of another kind, by smell or sound or memory. Am I listening to something rote or an act of exploration? Could I discern the patterns of dance steps and orbits, the choreography of an action hero, the joystick navigation left-left-right left-left-right of tunnels and tubes? What is the sound of a minotaur? What can you hear at the center of a maze? Light gets in the same way it does, my father says. Whatever hole or rent or aperture is at play, it pours through just the same.

I worry that Mortimer is trapped up there. What if this is the thump of protest? What if Mortimer got in when Mortimer was little and then got too big to escape? What if Mortimer fell through a patch of bad luck and can't climb out? What if Mortimer beamed in or teleported or time-traveled but there's a glitch in the system and no going back? My father is unconcerned. It has to eat, he says. His Mortimer is a forager, a commuter, a passing fad. My father keeps eating his breakfast. My father waves his hand. But my mother says maybe it lives on the honey—all those bees swarming the eaves of the porch these last few years, the same southern side of the house.

We all know treasures are hidden in dark spaces, in caves of one kind or another, and we all know treasures are guarded. Protected by dragons, perhaps. Or ghosts. In Texas the tales are of bee caves: the sight of smoke that turns out to be swarm, the seeker led into caverns and dazzled by such tempting golden walls, only a pool of water or a den of snakes away, but then the fire laid to smoke out the snakes getting out of hand, melting the combs, a molten desire, the treasured a thing that can only be witnessed and then lost, run away in a river of honey and wax.

In the old French, a *garrette* is shelter for a sentry, a place of support and protection. And I do not pause to consider, until much later, that Mortimer could be a guardian, a lookout, a keeper or a minder or a watcher. I would not have said we had an attic, much less a garret. I was a child while this house was constructed, acutely aware of crawl spaces and access points, lobbying hard for a dumbwaiter I could ride in or a hidden room behind a bookshelf or secret passageways connecting this and that.

There was a time I knew it down to the studs, without windows or doors or caulk to keep things out. I remember this house being built, its foundation dug, then poured, the stories without stairs yet to link them, the sudden miracle of framing, like mushrooms after a rain, how quickly it goes up, and though the pipes and the wiring will enliven the house, make it livable, though the roof and the walls will secure and define it, it is the framing which makes it, for the first time, seem real.

▲

THERE IS A SCHOOL OF THINKING THAT ITSELF SHAPED THE medieval world for a time, a belief so certain it may have been something else, was treated closer to a self-apparent fact that the world was made by a god and that god had left messages in it, stories, instructions, perhaps clues, hints, a great scavenger hunt of meaning, moral lessons in the nature of one beast, the very truth in another, the whole world coded in allegory, ready for the faithful to crack. Why else are walnuts shaped like that, if they aren't good for your brain? Look at this leaf like a heart! The sailors speak of pelicans, spearing their own feathered chests—you can feel it, can't you? The meaning? The world itself awash in sympathy and resonance?

I have named the unknown Mortimer. And suddenly I feel so tenderly about it. And from that leap, how quickly, how absolutely shockingly fast, does it go from a thing to a symbol. But of what? By turns it is searching, it is home, it is intrusion, it is displacement, it is warning, it is threat. It is belonging and invasion. It is change and always thus. In some cultures there is no tooth fairy but rodents come to fetch the human baby teeth dislodged from the head they grew in, marveled at held in the hand, and thrown up onto shingles or thatch for the mice to collect and take away. Maybe Mortimer is kin to that, come to take some childish thing, but I see it more as a swarm or a sweep, a haze, a weather. A prophecy? An icon? Something ancestral or archetypal or rooted in the earth.

It is an unknown thing in an unnameable space, traced while I am turned to face the celestial, an opaque veil between the heavens and me. My aunt Ellen, the bookbinder, says totems do not represent who we are but what we need. The longer I am its student, the more I question whether it has singled me out. I come to believe it is not listening to me at all. Certainly I seem unable to interrupt it, to frighten it off. But then I haven't lived here for ages. It is probably right to think it was here first.

↻

THIS IS HOW I BECOME A MYSTIC. THERE'S SOMETHING SIZ-able rasping and thudding in the space between the ceiling and the roof here in my childhood bedroom, a threshold, a portal, if ever there was one. I am much more fond of it now that I've named it Mortimer, find myself invested in its well-being, and as soon as I pay better attention what I can't ignore is how it changes again, how clap-your-hands fast it conjures more. I start trying to pick out the friction of tooth and claw, and like that I can't ignore the symbol and metaphor and myth—how else to interpret it? What else is suggested by the mysterious movements of the unknown overhead? What omen or prophet is this?

↑↑↑

I AM LISTENING ALL THE TIME NOW. I LIE AWAKE AT NIGHT. I catch it again in the morning. I hold my phone as close as I can to the ceiling and record. I don't know if it sleeps. I cannot tell what Mortimer is or represents or conjures or suggests. I imagine a badger, though we don't have them here. Which is to say I imagine the form of a badger, my idea of a badger, a thing I've never met but which I believe to have the requisite heft, possibly a taste for honey, the bristly percussive sweep of fur.

My friend the journalist wants to know what I think it is. I think Mortimer is a kind of mischief, a trickster, a shape-shifter. A premonition, a manifestation, a resonant string. The sounds I describe don't clarify anything, but for my friend, who has owned quite a few houses, who knows the scent of metabolism seeping through the walls, the direction makes it definitive. Opossums go down, she says matter-of-factly, raccoons go up. They can get pretty big, she says. I say it seems bigger than that.

My friend who illuminates manuscripts wants a portrait of Mortimer—asks eagerly, joyfully, What is the face of The Unknown? Our mutual friend who builds furniture and texts me old song recordings and images of mammoth ivory carved into a lion-headed woman, an icon eight times as old as written language, says he sympathizes, says he understands the urge, but we should stop right there. There are rules in this life, a few of which are precious to him, and that we never show the monster is one.

He hints we ought content ourselves that naming is enough. Naming is a way of owning, of knowing, and surely Mortimer is less annoying than Fate scrabbling around dropping Fate pellets. We cannot see the monster or Mortimer or Fate or the pellets. That is how it is. That is how it should be. You disturb the balance, you break the truce, you do so at your peril.

My friend who illuminates is unafraid that we will go too far. The Unknown, she explains, is unknown because it is a master at hiding. It is in no danger of being uncovered. It hides, behind a name, within an image, scraping the fascia board and dropping now-you-see-me-now-you-don't pellets at every turn. We may glimpse it, perhaps, we will know that it's there, but we will see what it wants us to see. All we can show is that.

I ONCE KNEW A MORTGAGE BROKER WHO WAS GETTING married and, among the relevant professionals, hired a metaphor consultant. What a title. What a function! I have wondered ever since why we don't hire them all the time. What could be more useful?

There's a kid two houses down from my folks, with a stand selling pineapple guavas, five for a dollar. I've never tasted anything like them and I've never had them anywhere else, the flavor so striking, my nieces already initiated, old hands casually explaining you can eat the skin but, as with a kiwi, nobody does, except my nieces, their chins already sticky, who aren't allowed or can't be bothered with knives.

My mother tries some one night in a fruit salad, but they drown everything out, shout everything down, a flavor like the me-me-me-me of a certain kind of precocious child star. Which is to say, they overpower. They don't make sense with anything else. The next day, we buy more.

Which is to say, wouldn't I stop for any revelation? Why is there no neighborhood stand with an honor box asking for hardly anything and a little basket of metaphors sheltered from the sun?

⇵Ŧ

A FEW DAYS AFTER I'VE LEFT, I CALL HOME AND MY MOTHER says the neighbors finally figured out their raccoon trap, the one I saw empty on the lawn, the one they said seemed only to attract the dog. Turns out the whole time it was upside down. Can you believe that? So simple. How easy to be turned around. Anyway, they righted it, and sure enough the next day had a raccoon in it. Oh, and the bee guys finally came to relocate the hive, the same day in fact, so there's that. Mystery solved. That humming eave is quiet now too. I'm not sure if the trap and the bees are meant to signify one explanation or two, but my mother is satisfied this is it. She is building to denouement.

In chess, there's an opening called the Mortimer trap. It had a heyday but now it's rare, a novelty, considered an inferior move because there are so many ways to respond. Probably it's a waste of time. Probably it risks too much, black in retreat, feigning error to tempt white into making a bigger mistake.

My mother says, as though the news will please me: she hasn't heard Mortimer since. I think she never wanted to hear it. I think she never listened as closely as I do.

Those who go beneath the surface do so at their peril.
Those who read the symbol do so at their peril.

—OSCAR WILDE

THE SORCERER HAS GONE TO ITALY

ONCE, THE SORCERER DROVE ME OUT TO THE OLD TURF house, next to the healing spring, and told me all the different ways to cut the sod to shift its purpose in construction. You can make one thing many. With enough effort, you can make a place to live. But if you neglect a turf house, the whole thing will collapse after just a couple of years, sink back into the earth it came from, gone—except the land won't forget all that living, all those people and their livestock penned in every winter under one roof, and for a century to come the site of that old homestead will be the first place in a pasture to turn green, when the light finally comes back and it's time again to bloom.

IT WAS THERE, IN THE NEXT VALLEY OVER, THAT HE TOLD ME about a sorcerer here a long time ago who had to escape his pursuers. I don't remember why. I remember our car was in low gear, climbing the narrow gravel road, the valley spread out behind and around and ahead of us, verdant, sun-drenched, but with clouds blowing in. He told me about that sorcerer fleeing up these same mountains, how that sorcerer called down the mist, and disappeared.

HE HAD BEEN A CARPENTER AND A BUREAUCRAT AND AN ACTOR, but when I met him, the sorcerer was running a museum. It was like he had settled into his final form. But even in that form he wasn't fixed. I don't mean always in motion, the way some people are, but always the center of some new scene. I'd go to find him and he'd be at the sink in the museum's kitchen or nested in papers at his desk or loading up the new kayak in the parking lot or sitting contemplatively at a picnic bench, staring out to sea.

EVERY TIME I MET HIM, EVEN FROM ONE DAY TO THE NEXT, IT was like the last time hadn't happened. There was no reason for him to remember the first visit, when I was just another traveler drawn there on a rainy day, gone again in an hour or two because there was nowhere in town to stay, the night spent on the other side of the peninsula, in a fjord so windy the sheets drying on the line stood out straight and by morning one side of the dirt-road-dusty car had been blown new-paint clean.

BUT ANOTHER DAY WE SPENT ENTIRELY TOGETHER, ON MY second visit, when I'd come back working on a book, a whole day in the exhibits and the archives, and when the museum closed for the day he made me dinner in its café, told me the Icelandic word for "television" translated to something like "oracle box," and I asked everything I could think of, took notes on it all, but when I returned the next morning to pick up the conversation, he blinked at me as though we'd never met.

ONE DAY I WALKED IN THE FRONT DOORS AND HE HURRIED me out the back, my stride never broken, just picking up speed, everything escalating, as he explained a whale had been spotted, I should go, pushed me into the last seat of a waiting car, engine running, driver shifting into gear, while he stayed behind and I sped off with the strangers to chase the story of a whale.

ONE DAY HE SHOWED ME AN INVISIBLE BOY. ANOTHER DAY HE showed me trolls. Two of them. Petrified, of course, caught in the sun's rays and turned to stone. There are a lot of trolls off the coast of Iceland, blocky hulks the stories say got distracted and forgot to retreat or hide or go underground, lived their lives in shadow or twilight or darkness until they were caught in a moment of haste or inattention or dumb bad luck and the light of the sun on their bodies transformed them, made them per-manent, towering here at water's edge.

ON MY THIRD VISIT, I RETURNED TO THE MUSEUM, ASKED FOR the sorcerer, and a man I'd never met had to tell me I was at least a year and a half too late. I remember the shock of it. The strike of it. The sudden confusion and sadness of it. Not just the death but the disappearance. A thing that has no language breaking my face into sobs. Or else it is a thing that has a language of its own.

I WOULD THINK LATER WHAT A WEIRD JOB IT WAS, ALL THIS summer staff, all these people who hadn't necessarily even known the sorcerer, having to break the news to some unknowable number of strangers. Maybe it still happens, years after the fact: all these people, one by one, forever finding out. I would think later still about the phrase they used among themselves, the one they told me about as a kind of consolation, the way they would say, "The sorcerer has gone to Italy."

THEY SAID IT BECAUSE HE HAD BEEN PREPARING FOR A TRIP when it happened. Among the rhythms of the year, he went away every winter, would have been on his way that very week, returning to a place he loved. The staff liked the phrase, I imagine, because it was such a gentle elision, hinted at what happened, kept the supposed-to-be version but layered over it another meaning, the phrasing so very much the way we talk about these things and so almost what happened that it was nearly kind of both ways the truth.

LOVE IS A JOURNEY AND LIFE IS A JOURNEY AND DEATH IS A journey, too. So much of our thinking is done in metaphor, so much of our language. We are forever making sense of one thing through another, saying something by means of something else, working it out like that: the vast and unfathomable translated through and given tether to the known. Just try to shake the idiom out of how we talk. Scrub it from our text. We can do it, but we become so limited, so hopelessly direct and concrete. Direct and concrete have their virtues, don't get me wrong, but we live by what sings.

THERE'S A FAMILY OF HOW IT HAPPENS, ALL THIS MAPPING OF resonance and relationships until something connects. We do it with symbols and similes, models and mascots, icons and idols, all these vessels and conduits, sometimes specters, sometimes doubles. Sometimes fable, sometimes embodiment itself. But metaphor in all its guises is not mere euphemism, no such gentle code, no, it is not a veil but the light itself: a way of seeing, of transforming, of bringing into focus. Even when it is another kind of optics: the filter, the mirror, the pinhole projection that lets us stare at the otherwise unseeable sun.

YOU SET THE BELL OF DEATH RINGING AND IT REVERBERATES, primes everything else to mourn. In an essay about a death, a valley becomes the valley of death, a house becomes that eternal home. We all become students in English class, trained to root out that symbolic key to unlock what everything really means. Is the traveler the grim reaper? Is the desk attendant a gatekeeper to the beyond? Is the mist tears or forgetting?

OUR HANDS ARE IN THE AIR NOW, BUT WHY WON'T THE writer pick one? Why is she still in some psychology class reading a couple of language philosophers making an argument about women, fire, and dangerous things? Why won't she admit this is about a thing she can't understand and an idea she wants to explain everything? Fine: it's about things she can't get over. It's about things that stick, immutable—even as it is about shape-shifters and stand-ins and the sometimes slipperiness of sense. We get it: this is an essay about death. The petrified troll is about neither stone nor troll but death. All these endings, all this erasure, all this loss—what else can it mean? Unless it is about resurrection? Wasn't there mention of a carpenter? Wasn't Jesus a carpenter too?

IT WAS SUPPOSED TO BE AN ESSAY ABOUT A PERSON WHOSE professional identity led to being known broadly as the sorcerer, about what it means to live like that, what it might mean to take that language at face value, and the legacy it leaves. And surely this intersection of what an idea can do to reality, this glimpse of each changing the other, surely it sets the stage to talk about conceptual metaphor, about how we make and find and uncover meaning? How could it not, with all this magic and travel and death? All this sight and vision, all this unseeable and dark?

BUT NOW THERE ARE ROCKS AND VALLEYS AND TURF HOUSES and forgetting and stick-shift cars. There are whales, for goodness' sake. And kayaks. There is summer staff and television. There is the palpable, the everyday, the mundane, so mixed in maybe you didn't notice—and the thinking by metaphor that is maybe the most ubiquitous commonplace of all, only it's so reflexive, so ingrained, so unblinkingly natural to the human brain we'd never notice it's the breath by which we live. We are so primed for proxy, for polyphony; what should really surprise us is something that keeps its meaning on the surface.

IT IS A THING THE ESSAY LOVES: TO TEND, CAREFULLY, PAINStakingly, to the fact of the world. Sheer material, corporeal existence, all its textures and interactions, what any of it is and how any of it works—is there anything more stunning? It is enough to witness it well, minutely, enthralled. And surely that is enough, more than enough, I'd bet my life on it, yes. But the essay cannot help itself. It wants also for that very fact, that insight, that mechanism so keenly seen in itself to be exactly that *and* be a symbol, an allegory, a metaphor, another meaning, too.

AND WHY STOP AT ONE? IN EITHER DIRECTION? MANY THINGS a metaphor and many metaphors to capture a single thing. Meaning itself twinned and twined in the mirror of metaphor, until we grasp at it as work product, as new territory, as hidden object. It is a dazzling multiplicity, such abundance, layer upon layer blooming out in expansive precision. Death is a journey but also a rest, a summons, a departure, a deliverance, a boundary, a reunion, an arrival, a fall. Death is also up. Death is an object and a person, a worker, a reaper, a dispossessor, a sweeper, a grim escort, and a thrower of objects into the eyes. Death is silence and sleep and winter and night. Death is the end.

METAPHORS THEMSELVES CAN DIE, BE DEAD, WHETHER YOU were taught that happens when they become conventional, so commonplace they trade like a commodity, without any of the spark of surprise or novelty, or whether you prefer the reading that a metaphor dies only when it falls out of use, maps nothing we care to know, lies still and unsummoned, its path to meaning untrodden and overgrown.

THE LAST TIME I WENT TO VISIT THE MUSEUM, I STOPPED ON the way. I stopped to see if I could find my way back to the trolls the sorcerer had introduced me to. It had been a while, but there was something about it that kept at me: the man who called himself a sorcerer taking me all the way out to see the rocks he called trolls. He was a storyteller, everyone said as good as they come, but note he wasn't content just to tell the story. Somehow it wasn't complete, just wasn't the same, without something solid you could touch. He told me on the way about all the sheep on the road, how you have to pay attention, how if you hit one you have to pay the farmer and you don't even get to keep the sheep. He didn't start to explain a thing about the trolls until we were right in front of them, until there was something undeniable I could see.

AT THE TIME THERE'D BEEN A BOX OUT THERE, HIDDEN AWAY like a magic trick, buried underground. When he'd unearthed it, the box contained a figurine and a key and a little notebook with a pencil to write your name if you found it. The key was unmarked, but the sorcerer told me which lock it would fit. I don't know if I wrote my name or felt I should wait until I found the box myself. When I returned, the trolls were just as I remembered, instantly recognizable, and I stayed with them awhile. But for all my looking, my prodding, my reaching back into memory, I could find no trace of the box. I could not tell you if it's even still there. But I know which door would open, if we ever find the key.

WHEN I GOT TO THE MUSEUM, INSTEAD OF THE SORCERER I met a woman with two beautiful children. She has the sorcerer's old job, but no one calls her "sorcerer" or "sorceress" or "magician" or "witch." I bet they would if she asked, but she doesn't. She's the manager. People call her by her name. We were watching her children watch a bird on the other side of the window when she told me something utterly fantastic and mundane. She told me she'd married the invisible boy.

I HAVE TO TAKE HER WORD FOR IT. I'VE NEVER MET HIM myself, haven't seen him to this day, though I've known his footprints in a vitrine since my first visit, the way they settled into stones still there to be seen, even now, unchanging since that first impression. It happens all the time: a thing you can't see known by the things you can. Of course that was a long time ago. Things change. The invisible boy had for some time now been a grown man. And these children about to run barefoot outside, into a gravel lot, called on by the darting of a bird they would only ever get so close to before it flew away—these were his beautiful children, too.

I CAN FEEL YOUR HUMAN FINGERS

Hundreds and hundreds were the truths
and they were all beautiful.
——SHERWOOD ANDERSON

JOANNA WAS THE PERFECT HEIGHT TO BE A PRINCESS, BUT SHE was employed as a chipmunk. She was glad when she got to work early, had her pick of heads. You might think the selection would be a question of mood or disposition, whether you wanted to be the prankster or play it straight that day, but really it was a very simple matter of how much weight you wished to carry, how awkwardly it would sit on your neck.

There are people who get their dream jobs, and Joanna's was to work in that kingdom. It was not a dream, or a reality, I would have guessed had Joanna not told me, later, far away in a bindery, as we sewed signatures taut. But then I suppose half

Fig. 2.ª

Fig. 2.ᵇ

Fig. 2.

Fig. 3.

⅙ n.

½ n.G.

Fig. 3.ª

Fig. 1.

Fig. 1.ª

Fig. 1.ᵇ

b

vergrössert
a

c

Fig. 4.

n. 6.

Fig. 1.º

the job was a kind of disappearing, avoiding suspicion or detection, even if the other half turned on being unmistakable.

Everyone in her division was sorted and distinguished by the sole characteristic of height. It's worth noting that the taxonomy of masked characters has nothing to do with good or evil, male or female, leading or supporting, old or young, human or otherwise. It is refreshingly free of dichotomy. One lives by the great constant of which costume will fit. There is no personality inventory or aptitude test. There is only the gradient of stature, steps that sort into whole classes of what you might be.

What you stepped into then was a new way of being. What you stepped into had whole cooling systems and strategic fans, protocols for feeling faint. What you stepped into included the day Joanna met a family and got waved into a Kodak moment. She bent her chipmunk knees and crouched down to better frame the picture, chipmunk paw in the hand of a very little girl.

This was an adorable child, hair in pigtails, who knew how to smile for the camera and at the same time speak through bared teeth. The kid, clearly adored, clearly the center of not just this tableau, spoke in the hiss of a whisper that would not reach the camera.

I can feel your human fingers.

As if blackmail might come next.

The chipmunk said nothing—Joanna said nothing—but perhaps in this moment froze, and not just for the sake of the shutter.

THERE IS SUCH POWER IN KNOWING THINGS. IT IS SO COM-pelling to tell. It is not enough to have a piece of information, we must set the air vibrating with it. The old bestiaries knew as much when they claimed: Lion cubs are born dead. They stay dead for three days, the bestiaries said, until their mother licks them and their father breathes life into them. The scribes meant the lion but also the divine father. They meant to say something about spirit and this mortal coil. They meant allegory over natural history, every time. But didn't they mean, too, that this is how it always is: the material fact of the world dead to us, every new thing dead to us until we have ways to make it mean something? To, as we say, "bring it to life"? And don't we, over and over, do that with our mouths, with the movement of our tongues and the shape of our breath?

Maybe it was just the distortion of speech through gritted teeth, but it struck the chipmunk as so purposeful, so malign, so totally creepy. It was a good story, later, in the bindery—I know that we laughed—but it haunts me still.

There's part of me that likes to think somewhere there's a whole album of such encounters, maybe not just in this little girl's family but in others, too, probably all stacked away, all but forgotten, but somewhere a document of fantasy after fantasy brought close and put on notice. Because wouldn't we just? Revel in our cleverness. Tell being after being we were on to them. Be sure, at all costs, to be nobody's fool.

I can feel your human fingers. Obviously, the child was not wrong, but this honesty was not refreshing. It was not the relief of disclosure or unburdening, a statement of fact spoken through a little screen, to a confessor confined in the vessel of a tiny sacred space.

Nor was it eureka, the joy of figuring something out. Neither was it the thrill of sharing a secret or the delight of being in on the gag. It was not the privilege of witness or the humility of discovery or any species of awe in knowing—for sure—*anything* at all. No, I think, just the opposite. It was not inclusion but rejection, not an expansion of the world but a contraction making it smaller. This was the sting, the delicious sting, of discovering a lie.

The chipmunk could not speak back, of course. Because chipmunks do not speak and it was not allowed, and anyway, what could you say? What was there to say in the face of a full-on power move, six words long, in which the chipmunk was outed, the jig was up, and magic itself was a lie? What do you say in such a moment, to such a child?

I mean, she was on to something. This was a chipmunk made up, then made by and made of human fingers. It was human fingers all the way down. And to the extent she was speaking truth to power, I say power to her! What do we suffer because we won't tell it how it is? I am rooting for every bit of autonomy and self-possession and standing up to authority inherent in this act. I am all for discovery. I believe in observation, that what we attend to will change the world. I think all those parts bode well.

But this child was not in the grip of epiphany, she was sending a message. She was a reckoning. Backdropped by an actual soft underbelly, she went straight to a vulnerable spot, and I cannot say if she did or did not know exactly what she was doing. There are so many kinds of innocence. But here I cannot help but see both: the righteousness and the cunning.

I don't remember who all read me fairy tales growing up, but it was my father specifically who liked to bring up "The Book of the Grotesque." Sherwood Anderson writes about it in a story of the same name: a book that was never published, penned by an old writer animated by his work and saved from the fate it describes because "something inside him was altogether young." The book suggests that in the beginning of the world "there were a great many thoughts but no such thing as a truth," goes on to assert we composite thoughts together to make the truths ourselves. To believe solely in any one truth, the book says, makes of it a falsehood and its believer a grotesque.

Maybe it's because I've heard it since I was young, part of the life my father breathed into me, but it still strikes me as correct. The folly of a truth too closely held. Indeed, the cruelty of a partial truth plays out again and again, there to be seen, an insult, a shard of it stuck under the skin. Which is maybe why sometimes when I think about the child and the chipmunk, I am struck that it is so very, bone-deep sad. It seems like a cycle that could be hard to break. We are terrified we can't afford to be taken advantage of. We like to be generous, but we fear our credulity. What a tragedy: we so hate to be taken in that we will pass up the chance to be taken with.

This child, so determined not to be duped, so set on getting her facts straight, so sure of what she could see and what she could feel, may have missed something intractable: it's not so singular. It's not even binary. We mix up the tangible and the intangible all the time. The world does not cleave neatly into abstract and concrete. We make meaning from metaphor, and we ask so much to be a vessel. If we are a tool-using creature, this is perhaps our favorite: the way we can make the physical hold the ineffable. My god. And sometimes back again. All tangled and entwined. We do it with language and story and tradition and ritual. Gloriously and incorrigibly, we do it all the time.

And maybe this is the least of it, but consider: there is nothing wrong with human fingers. What a ridiculous thing to have to say. Indeed, how astounding: they can be found even in chipmunk hands. Just as they can be found in a bindery, among punching cradles and the nipping press, rough-cutting parent sheets with dull knives, drawing linen thread through beeswax, deftly sewing with blunt needles, until a story has a shape, until a vision is married with language, until a thing has a story even before it has words.

The chipmunk holding the child's hand wasn't meant to defraud. No one was getting away with anything by working, within manifold limitations, to embody an ideal. To animate or articulate is so often to approximate, but if the gap between intention and substantiation is some kind of scandal it is also a marvel, a drop-dead absolute miracle, if any such thing exists.

I mean, what if we cooed it? *I can feel your human fingers.* We exclaim all the time at infants, at their little baby digits, fingers and toes at a scale we treat as unbelievable though we were once that size ourselves. How precious these miniatures, how tenacious the strength of their grip! The word we use is *perfect*, breathe it out at these creatures just come into being.

Yes, imagine if it had been a statement of tenderness. Oh, what love one might have for the bones that structure, the irreducible facts on which we hang all that imagination might conjure. *I can feel your human fingers.* I know you are there. I know this had to be made, fabricated, not like mendacity but like craft. Oh, how easily the tone can turn it. Change the lilt and right there, a statement of grace: "I see you, right to the core." Why wouldn't it be a relief to hear, in no uncertain terms, "I know exactly what you are"?

15

TED CRUZ IS A SENTIENT BAG OF WASPS

Why study the sheep when you can study the wolves?
—DR. JAMES PITTS

THE PARTICULAR MORNING DOESN'T MATTER. THE SPECIFIC precipitating news on the radio doesn't matter. The shuffling past me and muttering only matter because they were so casual, so mundane and lightly done, what might have been a throwaway comment said in passing, except that I think about it still.

One of the great delights of living with a scientist is that you can pose a rhetorical question—*Why are your hands always warmer than mine?* for instance, or, *Isn't it weird that we're basically* meat tubes, but within our meat tubes we have the ability to digest meat?*—speak it only to say *Isn't that something?* and then suddenly have an answer where it hadn't occurred to you there might actually be one.

One of the further delights of living with my scientist is the way a certain kind of science reporting prompts spirited yelling at the radio. *That's why we have controls! Correlation is not causation! Jad, that's just a bridge too far!* My scientist isn't one to insult, to get angry—not with strangers or people we know or the mysterious Reviewer 2—but accuracy matters. Protocol matters. You can have your metaphor, your *what if*, all the speculation and romance you like, as long as you're clear what you're doing. But you can't fudge the way science works or what science can claim, and we should thrill every time the scientist on record doesn't fall for it. And I suppose, tautologically, they never do, never accommodate or try to please like that, because if they did, we would stop calling them "scientist."

But this was not yelling at the radio. This was passionless. This was crossing the room with a cup of coffee in hand. This was no more than the caption under a scene, one no doubt sad and dispiriting but not overall surprising. "Ted Cruz is a sentient bag of wasps," my scientist was heard to utter. As if it were just one more bit of data on an entirely predictable curve.

● ● ●

I LIVE IN A COUNTRY WITH WHO KNOWS HOW MANY WASPS. Bee species number around four thousand, but I'm told wasp species are harder to count. It's likely no definitive list exists. Most people saying "wasp" are talking about a tiny subgroup, don't think for a moment that technically bees and ants are wasps too. It's a little like saying "mammals," a term that big, but a term so broad as to become amorphous. This is partly the difficulty scientists always face with common names, those things we would all agree we know but which we haven't formally defined, but even among scientists the taxon can mean different things to different biologists.

Still here we are, with the thread-waisted wasps and velvet ants. The great golden digger wasp and the noble scoliid wasp. The cow killer, reported to be among the most painful of stinging insects, lives in these United States. Here we are with all manner of wasps swarming to protect their nests, queens fattened up enough to survive the winter.

I grew up aware of the yellow jacket, of the way a bee could sting only at the price of its own life, which somehow seemed noble, but a wasp could attack again and again and again. I knew the yellow jackets just waiting to make a landing on the pull tab and duck into the soda can, half a dozen of them floating and wriggling and buzzing the aluminum walls if you got up from the picnic table long enough to make a sandwich. I was familiar with the yellow jackets curved as if to have as many points of contact as possible with the oak galls they crawled over, potato-shaped things in the litter of lobed leaves and self-pruned branches spread out under the two-hundred-year-old tree that was the reason my parents moved us there too.

Only rather recently did I notice the galls in my neighborhood here in Dallas, had to try and describe them, talk around them, until I knew the word was *gall*, even applied to these paper-thin spheres the size of a Ping-Pong ball, brown and bumpy as a toad, sometimes broken open—or hatched? I did not know—to reveal a cottony filament spread from the center point in fuzzy radii like one of those plasma balls toying with static electricity.

I was talking about them a lot that season, my new favorite thing, considered they might not be widely known if no one had yet pointed them out to me. But it turned out the impediment to my initiation was rather that they were too common. I described them over and over until some native son knew exactly, had the gall's name and its wasply origin at hand, was only thrown off that I had framed it as a marvel.

● ● ●

ONE COULD WORK THE METAPHOR. WE'RE TALKING ABOUT AN order of organisms characterized as either *stinging* or *parasitic*. Surely there's symbolism waiting to be had in the way solitary wasps prey on related species, a fact so salient we marquee it in the names of cricket hunters and cicada killers. We have the acronym WASP itself, and all the gerrymandering rigged to protect the territory of white Anglo-Saxon Protestants, as if they were endangered instead of invasive. I mean, novel behaviors do evolve, so let's even try to square Texas politics with the fact of a mated queen able to keep the sperm she's collected in something like a pocket, a testament to hive planning, electing when and whether to lay fertilized or unfertilized eggs, depending on whether she is at a point in her one year of life where it is advantageous to produce female or male wasps, respectively; females being preferable because they build everything and hunt everything and provide for the young, while males are worthwhile insofar as they make it possible for a female to make more females. Only the females can sting of course, the sting itself a modified ovipositor, and why even have metaphor and symbolism and science fiction if not to contemplate a reproductive organ evolved to paralyze, wielded by one sex only, capable of causing such pain?

Oh, one could perhaps suss out a specific species the way you might take a magazine quiz: Are you a solitary wasp or a social one? Do you see yourself in more of a lofty, elitist aerial nest or a bunker built into the ground? Is your venom more vindictive bile or toxic masculinity? Mostly C: You're a mud dauber.

But I did not stop to think about whether this public figure was more a bag of Mexican honey wasps or bald-faced hornets. I did not bother to note that at least half the paper wasp species found in this country can be seen in Texas—which is maybe an interesting way to imagine a legislator, the world transformed in their mouth until their legacy is built in spittle and fine cellulose sheets.

The point was not what kind of wasp but the bag of them, sentient, not unlike a few kids on each other's shoulders in a cartoon, cloaked in a trench coat and wielding brooms for hands, pretending to be an adult. I feel for these wasps, the bag of them, some kind of scarecrow gone awry, caught in that uncanny valley before they pass whatever the Turing test is for humanity.

Because, innately, I assume the wasps are trying. I assume the wasps want to do a good job. I don't know why being human is their aspiration, but if you consider where they started from, the learning curve they're working with, it's really very impressive what they've managed to achieve. And, sure, they have some work left to do, but goodness, they've clearly been at it for years, and who doesn't admire tenacity? Without even thinking about it, I assume they are still committed, that they're still trying to be a good human being, because why bother even trying to be human if you aren't aiming to be a good one?

⬡ ⬡ ⬡

I DON'T KNOW TED CRUZ THE MAN AT ALL. I KNOW SOME fraction of his performance, sound bites and appearances and commentary and analysis generated either in the course of doing his job or trying to get another one. I use his name and do not mean the person but the conglomeration of statements and positions and votes on the record that are the platform of his public life. Don't get me wrong—however much is persona or construction, chimera or phantasm, I feel the ripples of his speech very materially in my employment and my access to health care and the failed grid that should keep me and my neighbors safe and alive. But for all I know, he is a doting father and a nurturing boss and the best tambourine player you ever did hear. It should concern me that for all the faith and allowance I extend to the sentient bag of wasps, I don't credit the same assumptions to the man himself. That's on me. And yet, and still, if they were both on the same ballot, I'd be rooting for the wasps.

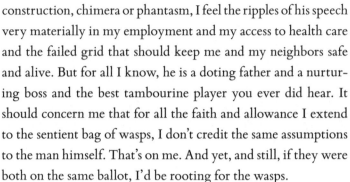

I TELL A CERTIFIED TEXAS NATURALIST MY THEORY, AND SHE says it has explanatory power. She says I have a very good point. But while I bring it up because the source of my new-found empathy, the very ease of its transference, has shocked me—bring it up because I am basically an alchemist, having found the secret to feeling tenderly about a famously unlikable figure; bring it up as a gift to others to unburden them of scorn; bring it up because I may have unlocked his *redemption*, even as I question my own—she means that what wasps know about us is probably unflattering.

What are we, in their midst, but violent, afraid, or indifferent? And if they are in any way wise to the fact that our species is making the world increasingly uninhabitable in almost innumerable ways? Sure, we've been known to plant fig trees. Maybe our eaves aren't so bad. But if the wasps just mirror back to us the way we are around them, do their absolute best impression from what they've seen, we probably fall somewhere between malicious and detached. And the wasps were already good at detached.

Most wasp species ignore one another, and they certainly don't think about human beings. Not the way they focus on spiders or aphids or plants. Perhaps we are mirrored in our indifference. Wasps will all but gaslight a human being until the moment we step barefoot or grab the unseen side of the door handle or otherwise manage to bring a wall of our naked human flesh to imminently smother them. Only in crisis does our species come to mind.

• • •

DR. JOE WILSON, A WASP RESEARCHER BASED IN THE BEEHIVE State, tells me, "*Waspy* should be a compliment." He doesn't mean a slender body and legs with relatively few hairs. He means a murder hornet is murderous only if you're a grasshopper. Even if you let one cozy up to your hamburger, it will just take a little divot, not even for itself but *for the children*—only the vulnerable young need that kind of protein. By the time you'd recognize a wasp as a wasp, it's reformed, a nectar-sipping vegetarian.

What he really means is that social wasps are highly organized. He dares to say, "You could call them disciplined, almost socialist in their sharing, working for the greater good." And yet, in the wasp researcher's experience, "In a bag, all that communal good goes out the window."

• • •

THERE ARE WORLD VIEWS THAT WE BEGIN BARELY HUMAN and progress towards goodness. There are also philosophies that we start in such grace and are corrupted, must find our way back. I am concerned for both of us that to humanize what I know of Ted Cruz, I need to waspify him first.

• • •

WHEN WE THINK ABOUT WASPS, WE ARE PROBABLY THINKING of that time we got stung at a barbecue. Which is a shame because we could be thinking about every fig with a dead wasp at its core. We could be thinking about the motherly act of stinging a tarantula, then dragging its immobilized body into a crypt to lay one egg on it before burying it alive—the sort of thing you can do because your offspring has the good sense to consume its host first from the appendages, the way you eat a gingerbread man, saving the vital organs for last because their very operation keeps the whole thing shelf-stable, gives you time to grow strong. We could be thinking of this most diverse group of insects—some of which are very big—in their hives with five members or two thousand, contributing to pollination and biocontrol, the very action of the insect world. We could be thinking about a plant's means of production hijacked so that a leaf plumps up in a decidedly not leaflike way, and we could be thinking about a tiny spider sacrificed, secreted into every chamber of a mud or paper comb.

We are hardly better with the subgroup bees, so quick to picture the black and yellow stripes on the Cheerios box, though many bees are gray, and some metallic blue. Meanwhile Yogi and Winnie and the very highway markers of the Beehive State have taught us wrong: all those depictions of humming hives fallen down like hapless helmets, the bulbous graduated tiers of icon, no bee ever made such a thing. They are the work of wasps. It's just like us, of course, to think we love a thing we barely know. And oh, what breathtaking twin capacity: to despise a thing exactly the same.

Twenty years ago, people who met the wasp researcher in the field would talk about their uncle who made honey or some memorable sting. Now they talk about colony collapse. They want to know if the bees are okay?

If we've achieved something of a public reckoning, a change of heart, if we've decided that bees are good and they're in trouble and we should help them, in that same span of time we seem to have doubled down against wasps. It's like we can't make a good guy without making a bad guy. That troubles me, deeply, the way it sounds so unsettlingly familiar. The wasp researcher ends every public lecture with a Q&A, and the two questions from the audience are always: "How do we help the bees?" And: "How do we get rid of the wasps?"

● ● ●

IT'S BEEN A YEAR SINCE TED CRUZ CHALLENGING ELECTION legitimacy was shortly followed by an insurrection storming the Capitol. Every wasp that was alive a year ago is dead. The collective being that is Ted Cruz should maybe be overwintering, but he is on Fox News backpedaling the word *terrorist* to describe the attack. It wasn't the right word, he says. How could he have been so wrong?

In a bough I've been watching from the water, on days the lake is neither too low to paddle its tributaries nor too high to squeeze under the footpath bridge that girdles the McCommas Branch, an industry of wasps have been building their hive. In the leafy season you could hear them, even before you drifted close enough to pick out the glossy brown sheen of carapace I've come to associate with cockroaches, their long thoraxes as if extruded from the cells they emerge from and build for others in turn. It's a weighty architecture at the end of the branch. Perilous. I have worried on fairer days about it falling into my lap. But this winter they've gone quiet, gone elsewhere as far as I can tell, have abandoned what looks like a heart against the sky.

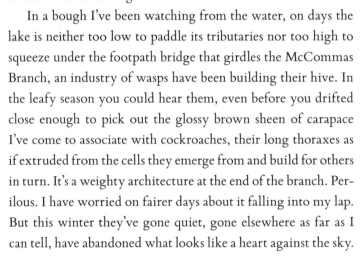

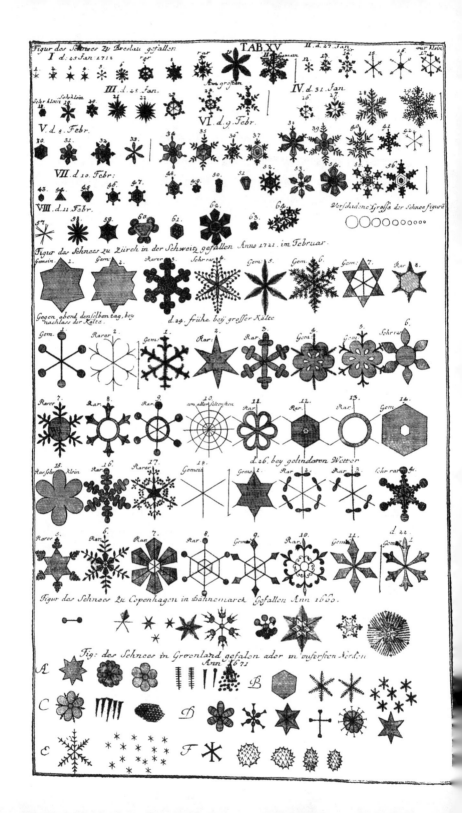

TAB XV

Figur des Schnees zu Breslau gefallen.

I. d. 25 Jan 1718.
II. d. 27. Jan.

III. d. 28 Jan.
IV. d. 31. Jan.

V. d. 5 Febr.
VI. d. 9 Febr.

VII. d. 10 Febr:

VIII. d. 11 Febr.

Verschidene Grösse der Schnee figure.

Figur des Schnees zu Zürch in der Schweitz gefallen Anno 1721. im Februar.

Gemein 1. Gem: 2. Rarer 3. Schr rar 4. Gem: 5. Gem: 6. Gem: 7. Rar 8.

Gegen abend, denselben tag, bey nachlass der Kälte.
d. 24. frühe. bey grosser Kälte.

Gem: 1. Rarer 2. Gem: 1. Rar 2. Rar 3. Gem: 4. Gem: 5. Schr rar 6.

Rarer 7. Rar 8. Rar 9. am aller seltensten 10. Rar 11. Rar 12. Rar 13. Gem 14.

Rar schwer klein 15. Rar 16. Rarer 17. Gemein 18. Gemein 1. Rar 2. Rar 3. Schr rar 4.
d. 26. bey gelinden Wetter.

Rarer 5. Rar 6. Rar 7. Rar 8. Gemein 9. Rar 10. Gemein 11. Gemein 1. d. 22.

Figur des Schnees zu Copenhagen in Dannemarck Gefallen Ann 1665.

Fig: des Schnees in Groenland gefallen oder in eussersten Norden Ann 1671.

A
B
C
D
E
F

16

BY DEGREES

But prove me what it is I would not do.

—ALFRED, LORD TENNYSON, "GODIVA"

SUNDAY I WENT WALKING. IT HAD SNOWED. WHICH IT
doesn't always do in Dallas, hadn't for a few years at least.
Everything was white except for the birds, who puffed up and
chattered from bare branches and left immaculate wire-thin
footprints an inch deep on the ground. I remember thinking
I had never loved this place more. The silence, the air, the blue
light of the sky reminded me of other places, other winters
where I had been overjoyed. Even in the ecstatic buzz of neon
dazzling over the doorway of a dance hall that was closed, there
was a tucked-in stillness of everything as it should be, and me
out alone in it, the only witness. And then, as if waiting for us
all to turn in, a few hours later, the lights went out.

MONDAY

I awoke to the morning chill of camping, though I was at home, in my bed. The library books I'd just picked up were all in arm's reach on the nightstand: another sign to stay put.

It is eerie for a room to go mute. There is a sound of a home without the thermostat rumbling, without the static of the refrigerator, the churn of the dishwasher, the tones of conversation streaming from the radio. Maybe it is just the sound of empty echo, or of blood rushing through your ears, but it is as if the pressure has changed. I'm not sure if it is the sound of what is always there, underneath, or if it is not even sound at all but the vacuum of its absence.

It seemed like a beautiful day outside. But, with the power off, it also seemed too risky to walk around in it and get colder—or perhaps first get too warm and work up a sweat and then be chilled as it cooled, wet clothes on wet skin. It seemed a shame to ignore good packing snow, the rare damp, clean stuff of proper snowballs and snow forts and snowmen. But it seemed too risky even to keep the windows uncovered and look out at the bright stark beauty of it.

I closed the blinds and pulled the thin curtains, which seemed ridiculous, diaphanous as they were, but one had to do something. I opened the taps to drip the two faucets. All the closet and cabinet doors were swung wide to warm the pipes. No one pities you for doing nothing.

And yet the wisest course seemed to be hibernation, withdrawal, a limiting. A this-too-shall-pass conservative approach. I put on a hat and some sweaters and read in bed, getting up only to add blankets. The headline on my phone said "rolling blackouts." The phone was old and because of the blackout hadn't charged overnight and the bad battery quickly went dead. The blackout stayed put. I organized my life to cling to what warmth could be had.

Having no electricity made some things impossible and others just more difficult, but a few things acquired new space, were suddenly available because so much was shut down. The burst of the blue pilot light catching to full flame was remarkable in the dark recess of the kitchen. I was with my partner, and the possibility of coffee and tea and steel-cut oatmeal stretched out before us. Each in turn was a victory. Already things had slowed, time had opened up.

Sometime later I finally pulled out the down parka from my Iowa days from its usual spot pinned against the far end of the closet. I went outside to sit in the idling car so that the phone would charge. I nodded to my neighbors idling in their cars, thought how we should arrive at a better signal, some surer way to know whether a body slumped in the front seat was a matter of huddling or exhaustion or poisoned air.

The car had been my grandfather's, the last one he bought, twenty-one years and two hundred thousand miles ago. The heated seats had broken before it was mine, and now the charger plugged into the cigarette lighter seemed overtaxed. The phone only charged a bit, but enough to text news to my family. Enough to find the internet and file with unemployment on my designated day. Enough even to look for vaccine appointments for the shot due that week. The check engine light blinked on. I turned off the car before the windows even had a chance to fog and went in.

I thought about an empty house down the street, how a few weeks prior the neighbor selling it said we could take anything we wanted, pointed me to furniture and serving trays and vintage berets and a vase made out of a shell casing and a whole trunk of holiday candles. A different decision and I could have now been surrounded by wax poinsettias and long red tapers, everything smelling like cinnamon.

Instead I heated soup in a seance of tea lights left over from luring out fleas. I ate dinner wearing two hats. I did the dishes and realized there was still running hot water, plenty of it, enough for a bath, which I took though I didn't dare wash my hair and let it dry in the frigid air.

The blinds and the curtains remained drawn. A small act that might make a small difference. Even as it seemed dangerous to close ourselves off—like we might never know if things were getting better. Each decision was like the head of a hydra, possibilities doubling and doubling, impossible to tell if we might suffer unnecessarily and if we might unwittingly make it worse. Outside, last I looked, the porch lights on the even side of the street were still ablaze. For all I knew, they had never flickered.

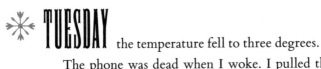 **TUESDAY** the temperature fell to three degrees.

The phone was dead when I woke. I pulled the cat under covers and he did not protest. I pulled the peace lily and the orchids farther away from their windows, could see already the leaves flopping and turning black. I knew that people who had outdoor plants had been bringing them in, but I hadn't considered it could freeze inside too.

I knew the back door wasn't always locked at the place a block away where I'd rented an office when I still had work. The unit itself had already been rented to someone else, but the building had electrical outlets in the doglegged hallway, in the open conference room, too, and I figured if I could get in, I could charge not just the phone but the portable backup charger and a handful of batteries for all the flashlights I owned. I couldn't call to ask permission, which gave me pause, but it seemed forgivable, at least explicable. I packed a bag with everything plugged into one power strip, walked over, found the back door open, and let myself in.

I tried very hard to look respectable, like I was supposed to be there. But even though it would have made me look more natural, I couldn't bring myself to unzip my parka or take off my hat. It seemed warm enough in the building—but what if it wasn't? What if I squandered my hard-earned heat? What would it take to get it back?

Waiting for the electronics to charge, I refreshed and refreshed the browser looking for a vaccine appointment, had decided to give up for the day when a friend on the same schedule texted to do it again, right now, that our health provider *was* offering vaccination but only today and only at one location.

Every county in the state was frozen. So many people were stuck at home. So many had fled. There would surely be supply chain disruptions and shipping delays even after the thaw. It seemed criminal to risk any dose going to waste. I continued my calculations: There would be heat on there, an accidental warming station, one of the few public places anywhere in the city that was open. The phone might charge some on the way over. It was only four miles there. It could be done by surface streets. The check engine light had only just come on.

The gate to my apartment building's parking lot was wired to operate by a motion sensor on one side and an electronic keypad on the other. Without power it had locked everyone in, but someone while I wasn't watching wrenched it permanently open, making it possible to leave. The car slipped a few times on icy patches. Most of the stoplights were flashing red or out altogether. I thought about my friend from the university who keeps insulated gloves in the car, not for Texas winters but to grip the searing steering wheel like oven mitts in the summer.

At the hospital entrance I pulled back my hat to expose enough forehead for the scanning thermometer to rule out a fever, and the automatic doors slid open. The nurse asked me with the curtain open if I might be pregnant or was planning to be so. I said, "Not yet," and I remember she said I gave her hope. She closed the curtain so I could wriggle out of enough layers to expose skin for the jab. No one cared if I stayed the fifteen minutes for observation, though I did. To be safe.

There is a particular adrenaline to driving no more than ten miles per hour. The brakes froze only once each way, that *chunk* feeling like there's something under the pedal, the vehicle slowing too slowly, never quite gliding into the brake lights of the next bumper but coming so close I couldn't see them over the hood. A block from home, I noticed the piles of belongings that mean eviction, on the curb, in the snow.

In the parking lot I nodded to two neighbors, idling in their assigned spots. Already the news had stories of people killed that way, poisoned by carbon monoxide. A friend of a friend had been taken to the hospital. In the twelve parking spaces, only those two other cars remained.

The downstairs units adjacent to the parking lot had been vacant for a while. I tried to remember if there was a correlation between their vacancy and when the eviction moratorium had lapsed. I had come to know the constable's car in the neighborhood, the paperwork sometimes tied to a door. It seemed possible that because the government and the property owners had not taken care of the tenants, let them stay, there weren't a lot of people left to take care of these apartments, to keep the taps trickling and ambient air circulating to warm the pipes. I don't know why those of us still there didn't think to intervene earlier. The doors weren't even locked, which we knew because lately they weren't quite pulled shut, left a gap to peek in, but somehow it just hadn't seemed our place.

That night after dinner, I was convinced to walk into one of them. Uninvited. With my freshly charged flashlight. Accompanied by my partner and the fear we would be caught. I was rehearsing an explanation in my head, in case I should suddenly need to provide one, and at the same time comparing the closet space and the kitchen layout to our unit. How rarely do we get to the interior of anything, it occurred to me, how little do we know about how other folks live.

In the one bathroom of the one-bedroom, one-bath, I pointed the beam of my flashlight down at the cold splendor of the toilet water frozen solid, as if an ostrich laid a diamond egg, its curves round echoes of the pot and the pipe, this bubble in the bowl like a glass paperweight, a crystal gem, the light filtered through the orb ghostly and miraculous like nothing I have ever seen. It was unearthly. It spelled disaster, but there was nothing we could do for the infrastructure by then but witness.

While the phone still had a charge, friends who had never lost power kept reminding us we could stay with them, at least come over for a meal and a shower. We kept weighing the risks: of the apartment, where we were now up to ten blankets on the bed; of the miles driving on ice; of traveling in the dark; of going anywhere in the car with the check engine light on; of not being able to come back; of breathing the air in the home of unvaccinated friends in the midst of pandemic; of trespassing on hospitality we might need more urgently at some later point. The quarters would be close and we'd have to bring the cat that was still half-stray and they were allergic and we worried we were already too tired to be decent guests, too drained to appreciate things and make conversation.

We knew there was some tipping point at which to leave. We knew we were close. But we didn't think we were there, yet. Our friends warm in their houses kept worrying, and we gave them the authority to make an executive decision. We gave them leave to tell us we were thinking with cold-addled brains and couldn't be trusted on this. We promised we would listen if they said it was time.

Falling asleep that night in the mute room we heard the rats skittering, maybe in the ducts, maybe in the walls, maybe in the space between the ceiling and the abandoned apartment above. My partner asked as a hypothetical if I'd rather be without water or heat. First things first, I said.

❄ **WEDNESDAY** the streets were still pristine. The temperature pulled from the teens to the twenties, and any dirt or dust or mud was still under ice or frozen solid, nothing thawed, the world encased. There were sometimes hints of tire treads on the surface, but the roads, like the sidewalks, like the lawns, like the roofs, were white.

House after house, the rain chains were frozen exquisitely, wholly enveloped, long and bumpy and clear like the plastic icicle ornaments I hung with my mother on the Christmas trees of my youth. Two streets down the robins were out in mass. There was a hedge shaken of snow and the robins were berry drunk, sloppy, hordes of them making a racket and a mess of the lawn. A blob of berry, in what stage of digestion I could not say, splotted on my chest, drew down like a medal, stained my parka immediately. I knocked off the worst of it, clumsily, fingers still stiff in my heaviest gloves.

It was ideal conditions for icicles, that threshold freezing point, and they were abundant, hanging from awnings and gutters and the corners of roofs, running one foot, two, *three feet* in some places. One could not help but be an admirer. I was tempted to collect them, a thing I had never thought to do before, but soon enough I knew the thin snap of ice broken free.

I saw an exceptional specimen suspended from the handle of a recycling bin on the odd side of our street, tapered to a tip just shy of the curb. It was fantastic, as if the blue tub had erupted a narwhal's tooth, and though I wanted to gather it in my icy bouquet, I spared it from collection. Some things are too magnificent. Some things belong to us all.

I knew the house. The kid there was five when the school year had virtually started, was six now, a thing that was easy to keep track of because they were the kind of family to get those special-occasion displays for the yard. We'd met the previous summer while the family was playing catch on the lawn. At Halloween they put in a candy chute from the second-story balcony to deliver sweets down to the socially distant trick-or-treaters on the sidewalk. Here in February they had just constructed an inhumanly tall snowman, with athletic gloves at the ends of its spindly stick arms and a football helmet sheltering its wee snowball-sized head.

This icicle sprouted from the dented lid of the recycling bin was fit to be the staff of an ice wizard, the stalactite of an enchanted ice cave, a frosty javelin if the snowman switched sports, was at the very least a testament to the teetering potential of melting point. It seemed wrong to rob anyone of such a marvel, and especially a child. The kid in this house, the kids next door who in better weather devised sweeping chalk murals on the sidewalk in front of their apartment building with the barred windows, the kids across the street in the blue house with their own snowfolk, and the ones from the house on the corner, all of us should know this very thing is possible. So I let it be, carried the icicles I did harvest like brittle kindling, learned quickly how fragile their crystal tips.

The entrance to our apartment building has two love seats flanking the big main door, like wicker lions standing guard outside with sun-bleached pelts. I tapped an icicle into the plush pith of snow on the one nearest my window, and soon the tapers radiated out like the halos of icon paintings, fanned from the frame like the poisonous spines of a lionfish, bristled from the seat like needles on a succulent. I thought it less of an ice sculpture than a kind of ephemeral garden.

I started out with the classic roof icicles, turned these needles and fangs pointy side up, but over time broadened my tastes. I pulled from wheel wells and bumpers where their tops flared out like cetacean tails, went after the ones that formed columns attached to the gutter. These I kept in their original orientation: knobbed like scepters or curved like scythes.

The water pipes, also at the mercy of freezing point, had burst and now began to thaw. From the back of the apartment building, water poured out of the wall and across the parking lot. I phoned it in, wondering how quickly the pooling moat would become an ice rink. It was surely the right call for the building as a structure, but it occurred to me when I hung up that it was less definitively in the interests of those of us still trying to live there. Indeed, maintenance was unusually responsive, the water promptly turned off to deal with all the busted pipes. As if in consolation, some hours later, the power came back on.

There were other transformations. The neighborhood café, shuttered since the first lockdown, opened its doors as a community warming station. We went over for coffee and the hot water to brew tea. We went to the bathroom and washed our hands. A family at the front table watched cartoons on a tablet. There were more people offering help than there were to accept it.

Food wasn't exactly our problem, but we decided there were so many pastries we wouldn't be depriving someone else. The staff said stick around for dinner, and we slid into our old booth in the back. They brought us takeaway boxes with medallions of pork and a well of yellow potato salad and steamed broccoli and carrots and cauliflower fabulous simply for being hot.

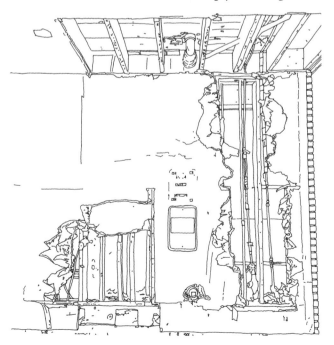

We hadn't eaten in a restaurant for a year. We felt both strange and familiar, cupped again in the red vinyl bench seats that never looked worn to the eye but the moment you sat down revealed their bumps and failings, unquestionably altered and broken down, grooved in the memory of all that had come before.

 THURSDAY the streets began to go gray, slushy. The walking was slippery, dangerously so, a couple of near falls in one block, the heart racing and the pace inching. But if the world was becoming watery, the taps were still dry.

We had bottles of water on hand but resisted using them. It could always get worse, and we could not estimate how much time we would have to bide. Instead, without any conscious decision to, we stopped taking in liquids. We ate less, too, in part because we were so sedentary, in part because time was indistinct and routine upended and nothing cued our hunger.

I started scooping the snow off the patio table in haymaker swipes, heated the first potful to wash dishes. A friend who grew up on the Gulf and never owned mittens or a scarf until she left the state had just been telling me that it's better to melt handfuls of snow at a time and not the whole pot at once. I cherished this bit of strategy, though I couldn't remember why it should work, turned it over and over like a worrying stone, something to hold on to.

The method offered something of the thrill of camping, of self-sufficiency and resourcefulness, of surviving after the shipwreck from the land itself. It had the pleasure of all deliberate, repetitive, conscientious tasks. We washed the dishes as meditation, with our artisanal, locally sourced snowmelt, and beamed at the clean counter in its wake.

The dishes were testament that we had already begun to eat differently. First we ate the things that would spoil without power, until we realized it was not so much warmer outside the refrigerator than within. Then we ate the comfort foods at hand. Then soups because they were so easy and so hot. Then we ate the things that would generate a minimum of dishes and utensils. Then things that could be heated in shallow pans after we ran out of clean pots.

Wood frogs, the world's northernmost amphibians, fill their blood with glucose and glycogen in winter, sugary as hard candy, and let most of their body freeze solid in the cold, not breathing, heart stopped—indeed do it a few times each winter before they sing their choruses of spring. Arctic woolly bear caterpillars eat what arctic willow they can in the brief growing season and then freeze, every winter for seven years, bit by bit accumulating sustenance until, eventually, they transform into moths that can neither eat nor survive a frost. What we were, what we were becoming, I did not know.

But things were in hand enough that I went to check on the neighbors. When the storm hit and the grid failed, they had packed up the dogs and gone to a relative's place. They'd come back as soon as they could, but they'd come back to burst pipes. They'd come back to a flood. The library in the front room was a total loss, and that was just what I could see from the porch.

At the door I could see Jim on his hands and knees in the foyer, picking up slabs of soggy drywall that had fallen from the ceiling. He stacked them like plates, filling another garbage bag. I asked if I could help, grab the broom at least. He motioned to the back. They'd left in a hurry, he said, unplugged the laptop from the monitor and the special keyboard and the fancy mouse and the printer and the backup drive. Now it was impossible to sort out what cords needed to go where to plug it all back in. His gesture said anyone could pick up after the sky had fallen; maybe I knew about computers.

Peggy was back in the office. She reminded me I didn't have to wear my mask on her account, that she could send me articles about why that barrier was bad for my health, but it was up to me. I wished I'd put my glasses on before I'd dropped by. I squinted at the cord ends and the ports on the various devices, picked up dongles like playing jacks. "We've lived here for thirty years," she said. "Thirty years. We know everyone on this block. They didn't lose power over there." She pointed towards the even side of the street. "And not one of them called. Not one of them looked in. Not one of them has asked."

When I left, I noticed, two doors down from them: the perfect icicle I had conscientiously left as a marvel the day before was already broken, dashed in pieces between the barrel and the curb, nothing if you didn't know what it had been. Such a small thing, so terribly unimportant, but what an icy straw on my back.

I felt my ethics of icicle harvest shifting. I no longer feared a tragedy of the icicle commons. I feared my priorities were wrong. Who knew who was even left here, sheltering in place, to share in this vision, in need of it? Life was for the living, and all icicles were fair game! The ones on the street, at least. Better that a vision be beheld and appreciated for sure, even by just one person, than leave it to fate as a gift to all.

By usual standards this was heady and excessive, but I felt very alive to the fleeting nature of things. Today was not like yesterday, was not like the day before. Each day one had to learn to navigate anew, answer the same questions for the first time, start over. After a year of pandemic—after a year of tragedies and protests and elections and trials, of insurrection, of things broken broken broken, of nothing like it used to be—we should perhaps have been used to that. But there are things you don't get used to. Ever and again, the issue was forced.

Throughout the day it was pointed out to me that my icicle garden looked a little menacing, had the aesthetics of a torture device. I know now that nobody looks at an icicle garden and thinks of its maker, either that it has one or that it could possibly be you. I'd pass the delivery folk or our mailman or a neighbor, and they'd say to me, like we'd both just arrived at this discovery, like it might not be true without someone to witness, "That's wild, isn't it?"

The landscape was already so different from yesterday's. Roof icicles, for instance, had become a rarity. I lowered my attention, ever closer to the ground and the gutter, snapping a crop of icicles off tailpipes and running boards and wheel wells of cars parked on the street. The sharp scythe shapes multiplied. The love seat grew gruesome.

 **FRIDAY** it was in the sixties.

The melting was in full effect. What snow remained in the shady courtyard was too close to the now pet-trafficked ground and too mixed in with leaf litter to be boiled into sterility with any confidence. But if it wasn't sanitary enough to do dishes, the snow was still at least waste grade, totally viable to heap up in the mop bucket and wait to see if we'd met that threshold quantity to flush the toilet with a great rush of snowmelt directly into the bowl. That plunge of water is both an act of physics and an act of faith. Even with good aim it risks either overflow or the job left half-done. So much is forgiving, until it's not. By such narrow margins do we skirt a very different outcome.

The café turned warming station was closed when we walked over midday. The folks inside said maybe they'd open after four. And maybe they did, but we didn't go back to check. We'd begun to feel sheepish. We didn't need warming. We needed the luxury of washing our hands, of a thermos of water for later, of not calculating when to use the ration of a flush that might not come again for days. That's not what they were offering. The warming station hadn't been open the two and a half days we really needed it, and somehow it was too embarrassing to point out how very much it helped to have access to something they weren't explicitly offering up.

We took the car to the mechanic. All their appointments had canceled, so they got to it quick. Which was a shame, because we didn't mind waiting. It was a place you could use a working bathroom, a place you could wash your hands.

That evening I considered if I should stockpile snow, just haul in bucket after twiggy bucket until I filled up the bathtub like a dam. The drain plug was good enough for the duration of a bath, but either it or the drain itself was not perfectly round so the fit leaked over time, surely would if left overnight, and I feared everything would just trickle down the drain. Nor did I know how much stray vegetation I'd be adding to the system, how much could be strained and how much might get stuck in the pipes and clog. It was one thing to have a problem. It was something else to risk introducing more while trying to fix it.

I brought in a bucketful of mostly snow. I woke the next day to regret, immediately, the modesty of my plan.

※ SATURDAY the temperature was in the seventies. Our water was still off, but it was a beautiful day for a walk, for anything outside really, and I stirred farther afield. There was a bit of slush heading up the side streets, a few slippery steps starting out, but all was clear sailing by the time I rounded the post office and came back down the grand, open boulevard of Swiss Avenue.

Everything frozen had melted. Everything, except where the snow had been unnaturally compressed, packed tight by human hands. But there was nothing incremental or in transition. The visible world was polarized into that strange stark binary of all or nothing. Which is to say whole vast lawns were drift-less and green, like there had never been a storm at all, the whole thing imagined, only every so often punctuated with the waking dream of six-foot-tall snowmen and bunkers for snowball fights and a snow fort even grown people could stand up in, fit with windows and ramparts and a flag, all still totally intact.

Contractors and roof repair trucks drove by, trying to make people whole. I saw a fleeting few plumber's vans on the roads, not even parked, always driving, like hummingbirds constantly in motion, as if they were too busy to stop. There was so much water rushing from one house to the gutter that I heard it a block away *glug glug glugging* down the storm drain. I stopped to judge how much I could catch if I went home for the mop bucket, whether there was time to come back and how many trips I could make before someone turned the key to shut it off.

When the softball-sized hail hit this neighborhood almost nine years prior, there were broken windows and dented cars and roof repair signs out on lawns for a year. Flash floods annually push up sewer grates and manhole covers, toss them aside as they make rivers out of roads and lakes out of intersections, a high-water line of silt and debris in their wake. Even when a hurricane farther down the pipeline causes runs on gas here, you may not feel it in the air but you can still see the lines at the pumps. The tornadoes, when they come, cut stark paths: old trees stripped bare, strip malls reduced to rubble and sky—and the next neighbor utterly spared.

I kept thinking about a certain kind of superlative bruise. I'm talking about the best ones, the spectacular ones, a display of every indigo and plum and mustard and dawn the flesh can produce. And I was thinking specifically about how, when I have one of those beauties, inevitably I never have the slightest idea what was the impetus for such a glorious mark, no idea how I came by such an inescapable token of what *must have been* an event!

This is part of what makes it the best bruise: the free ride of it, the mystery. It is all the pageantry and drama of *something happened* with none of the pain and suffering. I thought about the way I love that perfect bruise because I needed a way to explain a phenomenon precisely its reverse. Oh, you can have an absolute firework of an injury and not a hint to its origin, but you can also hurt yourself, quite badly in fact, and have nothing to show for it. Not a shred of evidence. At least nothing on the surface.

The neighborhood from the street is something like that: all the appearance of status quo out in the open, structures seemingly intact, with all the trauma and the falling apart unraveling behind closed doors.

There was something truly perverse about it, about how beautiful the day was and how absent the evidence of what had just happened—what was still happening—how it looked like everything was over, everything was fine, not even fine but *picnic weather* fine. It did not feel like a mercy, a consolation, not when so many people across the state still didn't know when they could go home, when we didn't know yet if we'd have to leave, when the official number of storm-related deaths was still ticking up, and the estimated number was devastatingly, heartbreakingly worse.

 SUNDAY, the week come full circle, there was still no bath taking or dish washing or laundry doing. There was only the cache of one precious bucket of melt about to be the last foreseeable flush. Meal planning revolved around whether one could eat without using hands washed mostly in liquid soap while also rationing the last of the clean utensils.

The plans I was starting to make were not about catching up from a whole lost week but the bare contingency for how to be presentable for a single Zoom event later in the week, now that nothing seemed to be closed or canceled, the storm and the cold blown through, the skies blue, the senators back home, the grid mostly running, and the governor trying to distract us from what we had seen with our own eyes, felt in our bones. But if chores were a shambles and generally indoors was an inventory of what was lacking and what was in excess, outside was again entirely lovely and mild.

I opened the windows for a breeze. I turned on the radio. I folded up blankets and put away the costumes of cold: I returned my parka to the closet and my coat to its peg and the hats and gloves and chunky scarf to the little storage tub of winter things. I thought about the mop bucket, now empty, resting in the bathtub for the first time in days with nothing to melt.

I went out and retraced the previous Sunday's walk, the walk I took when the snow was new and the lights were on and I was so uncommonly happy. It's a few miles out to the hospital and past the cotton gin factory turned condos and back around the bus yards and through the looping paths of the new park next to the elementary school. I kept an eye out for construction sites, for public toilets of any kind. It was time to scout.

The whole route, more than an hour of walking, I saw exactly two vestiges of snow. There was a blackened crush of ice and gutter muck pushed up against a telephone pole on a shady side street, and there was the last lump of a snowman on a lawn midway down my block. That was it. Otherwise, there was not a trace of the snowfall, much less the freezing cold.

We did not yet see how all the palm trees had died, whole walls of ivy perished, succulents slumped, shrubs and grasses and all sorts of plants turned the color of straw, bleached of life, blank and uniform, though the old hands cautioned you couldn't always tell what was gone and what would come back. They said be patient. They said don't start tearing down and digging up just yet. They said wait a few months to be sure.

The lot across the street had been empty when we moved in. From the window framing my writing desk, I had watched its weeds grow. I watched a sign say the property was sold. I watched a house be built. I walked through empty rooms at the open house, then watched the moving van come in. I watched a woman about my age weed and get the mail and head out for a run. I had meant to introduce myself. I would have loved that when I was new, a *neighbor*, remembered still what it was to move to a place where you knew exactly one person.

But the tenants moving into my own building never brighten when I introduce myself or offer to carry a box or tender my phone number in case something neighborly comes up. So I'd never introduced myself to the couple directly across the street. It seemed too far a distance, too alien an act—an impulse wholly natural to me but which would reveal me to them as a life-form perhaps to shrink from, both eccentric and without boundaries. Then they'd have to feel awkward if they ever noticed me as I sat at my writing desk, staring out the window through the open blinds.

And now it was too late. Much too late. They had been there for years. The runs had become walks with a newborn had become runs with a single then double stroller. It was definitely too late now that I was so distant from equal footing, so very wanting, preoccupied with need for something as basic as water. It was too late to appear at their threshold, to ask for a favor they could easily grant, my hair unwashed for some time. The side-street snow I'd seen had looked so hard, so frozen solid. It would be wise to take tools to chip at it, maybe plan for multiple trips the four blocks and back, which wasn't necessarily a deal-breaker, but its coat of road tar and particulates suggested more impurities than were wise to introduce to the system. It might have been a mirage. It might do in a pinch. But it made it hard to write off the more promising donor.

There was also the snowman in front of the blue house with white trim—or what was left of it. At the height of its powers the snowman had been towering, the precipice of what hands can reach up to build, but even reduced down to its derrière it was still a pretty sizable hunk. Even what was left of it altogether a better candidate. The snow was surprisingly pristine—especially for something left for days in the yard, and especially for something made by the hands of children. It was a mere five houses down. And it was on the even side of the street, which maybe shouldn't have mattered at all, these houses with their pipe integrity and porch lights eternal, but maybe that was also the tipping point.

I finished that walk with an unexpected question: Can you steal a childhood memory, swipe it right off the lawn?

I muddled through versions of this concern for the better part of the afternoon. I mean, even thieves have a code. Surely pilfering knows some bounds and one of them is robbing a snow bottom. Surely you cannot just take a tuchus. Surely you cannot slink off down a side street with a sleet backside. Surely you cannot tiptoe away with a powder posterior, and surely you cannot purloin a snowman haunch. Surely you cannot, under any circumstance, pinch an unnamed stranger's frosty butt.

Surely, to do so is a kind of kidnapping, of wonder and innocence, along with the weather-dismembered rump.

I thought how fundamentally strange it was that anyone owned water at all. I thought, too, about my pride, my ridiculousness, the four bottles of tap water I was hoarding in the refrigerator. I thought about how Christians and communists both arrive at the gospel "From each according to their station, to each according to their needs." I thought about how every day since the storm had been an adaptation. I thought about what was evolving. A week of constant weighing risks and making do was changing me. What had to be done? What could I get away with? What version of myself did I want to live with?

Questions of *whether* to take the snowman butt turned to questions of *how*.

Clearly it should be done at night, at an hour when one could assume at least the children were asleep. Adults would have their own questions about the shadowy figure on the lawn, posed their own problem in my scheme, but I didn't worry about traumatizing them. I worried about the danger they posed to me, but I was confident we could keep the innocent out of it.

The snow could plausibly have melted overnight. Which is to say narratively it wouldn't raise suspicion to wake and find it gone. The time line would fit. Hopefully this would minimize disappointment and distress, but also, time was not on my side. Decisions had to be made. As with the perfect icicle specimen, and the snow in the courtyard, and the warming station café, I suspected the option of one day would be gone the next. I went back outside to case the joint.

The snowman I intended to appropriate was farther from the sidewalk than I'd remembered, more squarely on the lawn. I wasn't sure if the house had a doorbell camera, but I imagined how the whole encounter would read from a fish-eye lens. The whole thing seemed suddenly cinematic. All the world's a stage, and all the men and women merely players. One has responsibilities to an audience that one does not to property lines.

Imagine a porch pirate dressed as an actual pirate. Imagine garbage collectors come in costume, perhaps the magician's tux and tails, treating your castoffs as props in little disappearing acts. Imagine something rare as a sasquatch snatching your lawn art. Imagine the silhouette of a myth gracing your front yard. Would you mind the loss of any temporary possession if you could say the Loch Ness Monster took it?

All of my problems now hinged on what to wear. Of course, too, my timing and my movement and the drama of it all, but first what I looked like. It seemed wise to err on the side of whimsy, to be eccentric but benign. I regretted that there was not currently a long sea-green tutu in my closet. I calculated how long it might take to fashion wings. There was a time I was quite handy with papier-mâché—it would require me to track down a hair dryer, but maybe I could make a mask in time.

These interventions seemed capable of such amelioration. I suppose context always does, but who wouldn't make the trade gladly: a thing you didn't need for a story no one would believe? Yes, one might haul off a snowman caboose, but seed a vision where it sat.

At nine that night there were still too many people out walking their dogs. The lights were on at the blue house from every last window, upstairs and down, the family collected in the living room, the curtains not yet drawn. I went back home, finished writing a long-shot application, submitted it by grace of the grid back up and running. I went out again at midnight.

There are a few reference points for creatures collecting scraps of youthful ephemera and spiriting them away under cover of darkness. I might have fashioned myself a puckish trickster, a Peter Pan. Or an incarnation of Robin Hood, redistributing wealth. I preferred to imagine myself a kind of errant tooth fairy. I wondered if I should leave a quarter. A dollar? Five? The going price of a tooth or a bag of ice? But it was not clear where to leave such a token or how to explain the transaction, and maybe framing it with a note would put it all in the right light or maybe drawing attention to the breach was the real misstep. There are a lot of things we'd rather not know, a lot of things that would be a gift not to deal with.

When I picked it up, hefting it for the first time, the rough globe of snow was lighter than I'd expected, probably a bad sign that what moisture was left in it would be meager, though for now the volume was still quite a bit larger than the mop bucket waiting empty in the bathtub, would more crown it than fit into it, like a scoop of ice cream perched on a cone.

I held it, I'm not sure why, at arm's length, as if I might do reps with a medicine ball, as if the slow song had caught me off guard at a middle school dance. There was ceremony but no gravity. I felt as if I were very formally delivering a beach ball to the queen.

And this was as far as I'd imagined: taking possession. The heist was no more elaborate than that, and yet only begun, the whole getaway before me. Departing by paved path seemed less trespass than escaping via the dewy lawn. People feel strongly about their lawns, don't they? Lawns are for children and animals that belong to the house, and for scaring off children and animals that don't. But strangers with some purpose have license to venture right up the walk, however welcome their packages or sales pitches or census taking. I tried to align myself with the strangers.

I stepped from the lawn back onto the concrete walk. I saw my own wet footprints trailing me and recoiled. Rookie mistake! Thoughtless. Of course we inevitably leave some trace.

Had I planned ahead I might have used it to my advantage. I could have made a point of leaving the three-toed tracks of a giant penguin, like the 1948 hoax in Florida, planted with huge iron feet. Not for nothing, I am the right height, if 34 million years too late, to be New Zealand's long-lost *Pachydyptes ponderosus*. Or better, I might have summoned enough regional pride to mimic the theropods and sauropods stepped into fossil record 112 million years ago and not two hours down the road. I had seen the potential for narrative, for story, for spectacle in this mission, but I hadn't even considered this exercise could be educational.

My instincts were only to get out of there, to beeline before anything more could melt away. But faced with the telltale tread, unable to undo what was done, I turned with drum major precision. I made a scrupulously orthogonal path. I took care to walk the straight and narrow down the garden path, then three shallow steps to the sidewalk, and directly into the street. The dark and uneven asphalt would obscure my tracks, I thought, like stepping into a river to hide my scent. I made one more pivot and stopped. I stood there, out in the open, in the middle of the street, halfway between the even side and the odd, holding the last physical trace of that storm that had set so much in motion, that froze so much in place. By morning, even this would be gone. I tried to collect myself. I marveled that I seemed to be alone, under an open sky.

Only then did I obey the urge to turn homeward. Only then was my trajectory known. I traveled right down the middle of the street. There was something very ceremonial about the posture, something very parade-like about the route. Like a one-person marching band, I thought, a one-person float.

In Texas the tradition of homecoming corsages has evolved from a single stem of chrysanthemum to a veritable sandwich board of ribbons and boas and sequins and lights. A girl decorated until she is her own float. The mums are still worn, but with more rigging than a single pin, adorned with stuffed animals, sometimes sound systems, constructions so elaborate Lady Godiva could be underneath in chaste procession and no one would know.

When I think about the Texas high school students shrouded and on display at the same time, I can appreciate both the need to be seen and what it means to have something—some facade, some shelter, some getup, some pretense, some tradition, some story—to hide behind, to take refuge in. When I think about Godiva, that makes sense to me too.

The actual woman has been more or less forgotten. Though she was documented in her lifetime, she has been trailed for a thousand years by a story not exactly about her, but maybe not unrelated either, the story timeless because it is a story about needless suffering—the story also about the outrageous, humble ways we might relieve it.

I see enough versions of her naked ride in art history that I start to think of Saint George and the dragon: iterated forever, these riders on horseback, set out to make things right. Though perhaps my favorite, a marble figure just two miles away in the art museum, has horses rendered only in the hem of her garment, has undone no more than the eagle clasp at her hip, because she is depicted at the moment she takes a quip as a bargain and accepts her challenge. She has the lifted gaze of martyrs and saints. The sculptor, Anne Whitney, also rendered abolitionists and suffragists, made this Godiva sometime during the Civil War though it was lost for more than a century, returned to the public record only when another woman, an art historian with a keen eye, spotted her, unexpectedly, in a Massachusetts backyard.

There is a version of the legend where the pious noble-woman is clad in silk for her ride, cut and colored to look like her own skin. I like that, the vision of her slipped in the work of silkworms not yet moths, the way it puts her on the precipice of chrysalis, itself another shelter, another sheath. The story itself is a thin garment, a way to contain and reveal, worn again and again so that we might grapple with dire straits and flagrant acts and how we might spare one another.

The relevant garment, lost in translation, would likely have been the simple shift of penitents, worn for the way it signals humility, that base layer of clothing never meant to be seen. Historians discount the whole thing, of course, are suspicious that the real woman and even the earliest version of the story now attached to her name are separated by a good two hundred years.

There is an altogether different story, something of a counterweight and almost certainly a fabrication, about one Madame de la Bresse leaving in her will a small fortune of francs for the singular and express purpose of clothing the snowmen of Paris. The story is of course delicious because it is ridiculous, charming until you imagine all the actual people shivering and then what a waste. I don't know why we are inclined to invent a prude or an exhibitionist, except we love a spectacle. There are various mechanisms of transgression, of crisis and change, just a few of which I believe I understand.

But I can see how a thing gets out of hand, takes on a life of its own. Some things, of course, happen like flipping a switch. One thing and then another. But so much comes about by stages and steps, cumulative and incremental, bit by bit, drip by drip, a relentless wash of gradients and waves, the situation fluid, swept up like an exponent or tumbling down in descent, whether gradual or rapidly escalating, like your eyes adjusting to the dark, like a snowball picking up speed.

FLIP

THE BIKE MECHANIC WAS A ROMANTIC. HE SENT ME A VASE,
then bouquets of flowers to fill it. He wooed me with itineraries,
written with a typewriter on onion skin paper, tucked in with a
little box of seashells, enough to tide me over until I could join
him and pick my own. When I did, I packed a ball gown, red
like the vase, and wore it one night, windswept, alone at the end
of the pier, waiting for the ferry to return him to me.

I had worn the ball gown to a fancy-dress Oscars night and
to a series of Halloween parties where no one found it clever
when they asked what I was and I said Miss Scarlet, in the living
room, with the rope or the wrench or whatever oversized prop
I lugged around all night as if I were a game piece. But I owned
it in the first place because I once spent a year in pursuit of the
right silver dress to be maid of honor.

There were no other attendants to coordinate with and the
bride wasn't picky, didn't care about these things, but it couldn't

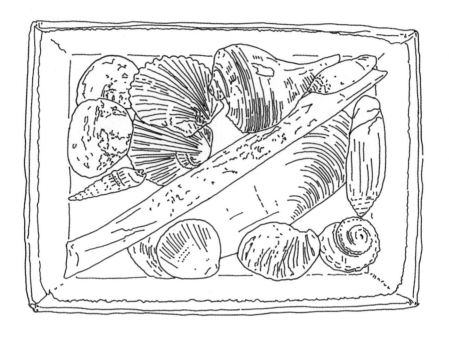

be sequined or shiny or gunmetal dark. Not gray but *silver*, and not disco ball silver, no, silver like metal, not mirror. The brief seemed straightforward, but as the wedding drew near and nothing passed muster, I figured I could afford the insurance of a backup from the sale rack, entirely the wrong color but cut like it was made for me and so cheap I could risk it.

I had found the perfect dress months and months before. I came out of the dressing room and the bride and I both knew, would have walked right out with it still on, except the sample dress was champagne, with an ivory sash, and of course the bride was set on silver. I had seen all the swatches of possibility and I told the clerk I wanted to order this exact dress in the silver. She said fine, but she needed to take my measurements. I said the dress had a size, my usual size, that all I needed was to change the hue. She said you couldn't trust the sizes, that the sample dresses got all stretched out, and I said then I'll stretch it out in silver, but she already had a measuring tape in her hand.

I don't remember the industrious intimate act of the measuring, but I know exactly how she looked at the numbers on her clipboard, looked at me, looked at the figures, said in disbelief, helplessly, "But you *looked* trim." Her face puckered in confusion and dismay. She would not sell it to me unless I ordered two sizes up, and I would not hand over a cent to someone who now looked at me as if I had deceived her, as if I had posed as a woman but was actually a whale. I didn't mind that I was a whale, would have been glad to live in the ocean and flip my tail and breathe out of the top of my head, but I wanted to be a whale in a dress that fit. I was not a whale with time to fly back for a fitting, nor was I a whale willing to pay for the privilege.

The bike mechanic, later, on a different coast, a few years after I was outed as a whale, believed we all need a bicycle. He would donate the labor if I picked up the parts. Even after we

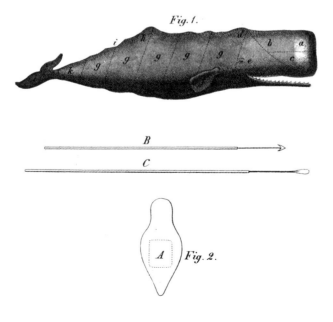

broke up, there was still the offer to build one custom for me—
the offer may yet exist, an immortal constant, a pledge, not a
favor, nothing merely personal but some kind of right.

The bike mechanic took me to his place of business and told
his boss I needed a fit kit. A fit kit is a piece of paper with a few
blanks to record a handful of measurements so the lift to the
seat and the lean to the handlebars and the stretch to the pedals
come out right, make you efficient and comfortable and safe.

My sister once told me about an Olympic athlete: recruited
to a sport she'd never heard of and thus pulled into the elite
levels of obscurity by a scout who had determined the ideal
physical proportions for it—and then looked for athletes who
had them, regardless of what they already practiced or played
or knew. It stayed with me a long time, this vision that you
could be perfect for something and not know, not even know
that thing already existed. That there might be someone looking for you. That maybe you could be discovered, your destiny
revealed, that there was already something, somewhere, somehow you fit.

I'd seen a glint of that once from a philosophy professor,
when I dropped by office hours to ask about the major and she
said in a placid purr, possibly drumming her fingers together
like a Bond villain, "I've been expecting you." And here was
maybe some new relative of that recognition, that falling into
place: how the bike shop owner looked at me, clipboard in hand.

Except it was like he couldn't believe it, like he needed to run
the experiment again and see if he got the same results, like he
had heard about a unicorn but never seen one, like theoretically
a black hole should exist but how would you know, like it was
too early to publish but my god what if the numbers were right?!

He kept looking at the clipboard, looking at me, waved
the bike mechanic over as if to witness, to confirm. The bike

mechanic did exactly the same thing—looked at the clipboard, looked at me—until at last they looked at each other, seemed to agree it must be possible, they just had never seen it before.

"Your femurs," they tried to explain. Had anyone ever noticed? How anomalously out of proportion, how advantageously out of proportion, how long and perfect a lever, how very built to power a bike! They seemed unable to believe I walked amongst them, how perfect my disguise.

Of course the ancestors of whales used to walk on land, too, hips a cluster of bones fused together. Of course they kept those hind legs, in one form or another, still functional for more than ten million years after they slipped into the sea. Of course even now whales have hip bones and femurs, set snug, wholly encased, in the meat of muscle. Vestigial, we say, but nothing we keep is without meaning.

Of course the bike mechanic and I parted ways. Of course I still have the vase and the little box of shells. Of course the night I waited for him on the pier the ferry came in and I watched every passenger disembark, watched the crew start to tidy up and turn out the lights before he finally emerged, still drowsy and disoriented, having slept, perhaps dreamt, through it all.

Fig. 1.

Fig. 2.

TO ASHES

WHEN MICHAEL DIED, WE STARTED BURNING THINGS. IT WAS Brian's idea. I had been asking questions about the chainsaw, how to get the teeth running smooth, and then Michael died and Brian figured as long as he was coming out to the ranch it might be fitting to get a bonfire going. It was finally cool and damp and still enough, and we had all the downed cedar from the summer, back when the drought got so bad the oak trees started to wilt.

I didn't even know oaks could do that, and I grew up in a landscape like this during a drought that lasted far longer, but we just had the oak and the sycamore and the pepper trees and the cacti back in California, the usual chaparral scrub. Cedar I guess changes the equation. Thirsty stuff. There are spreads around here where the folks cleared it all out and springs bubbled back into existence, water flowing as if from nowhere.

Michael and I had been rescheduling a walk for months. He had some places he wanted to show me. Down by the log cabin, I think, but maybe out towards the rusty cans and empty bottles of the old dump. But then something would come up last minute. The dog had a limp or his wife had the car or someone was sick and we'd push back until he could, as my aunt Billie liked to say, get his oxen out of the mire.

Instead of the walk he'd call. He'd call and explain how sometimes he just froze in place, that he didn't want to frighten me if it happened on our walk. He'd call and say that he wouldn't fall, exactly, that wasn't it, but sometimes gravity would just take over, and he didn't want me to worry. He said he was retiring, not because he was ready but because it was hard on other folks to be around him, and it almost broke my heart. He called and said he wanted to walk the ranch "one last time" and the phrasing struck me, at the time, as excessive.

There is no ritual like fire. It's absolutely consuming. You feed it and it transforms and then it dies down, rash and insatiable, a thing both responsive and uncontrollably wild. Up in the house the timber mantelpiece is carved to say "We sat down with Earth's greatest Philosopher—the Fire," and I appreciate the tale I've heard about the writer who put it there being the kind of person who loved a fire so much he'd run the air conditioner just to stand its heat on a summer day.

You don't burn cedar in a fireplace. The oil would gum up the works. Down in the burn pit, though, you can make a study of its combustion. The dry cedar needles start rusty red and curl white, skeletal, in the flames—and then they're gone. The green needles are almost as fast. The smell is light and clean, though of course the smoke can irritate the eyes. The needles go and then the branches go and then you push the trunks all the way in, a feathery bed of ash sometimes left like a shadow or an impression of the bough, then the embers stirred, glowing like memory, and that delicate impression vanished into coals.

We burn our grief. It feels good to run the saw and drag the limbs and loft them just so into the stone ring of the firepit. It's good to have purpose, to have something physical to do. The occasional scrape or jab by the cedar spines—that manageable, specific, locatable hurt—that feels good too.

I tell Brian I've been thinking about how once, when we'd only just met, Michael told me to call if I needed anything. Told me to call in the middle of the night if need be, that that was sometimes the most important time to call. I never needed to, so I didn't, but it was such a poignant offer. I'm not sure anyone else has ever said that to me, and now I wish I had called, while I could. Maybe it shouldn't stop me, knowing no one will pick up.

I tell Brian how Michael said there was something in the house, and that if I didn't find it on my own, he'd tell me what it was. I thought I'd figured it out when I discovered a little vessel that used to hold someone's ashes, a pretty wooden box squirreled away in one of the drawers of the credenza, a note tucked inside about keeping them until the moment struck you in the perfect place, the little bag empty and the whole thing sweet, I thought, but when I told Michael, he said that wasn't it.

I tell Brian how I think the narrative dictates that I'll figure it out just before I leave here, that in that moment it will all make sense and I'll be consoled, but an old friend up north says that's only true in fiction. She says Chekhov's gun never goes off in nonfiction, and she's sorry but I'm an essayist, which means I'm never going to know and that's going to have to be its own kind of consolation somehow.

We've started to pack up the chainsaw, put everything away, when I tell Brian about the turtle. I was up at the top of the property a few days before, back when Michael was alive, making

Juniper.

...n & Manchester R. R.

...FTER MONDAY the 5th of Nov.
...wing Schedule will go into effect on
...ton and Manchester Railroad.

EXPRESS TRAIN.

...mington daily at...... 4.50 A. M.
...Kingsville " .... 3.30 P. M.
...ingsville " .... 1.45 A. M.
...Wilmington daily at ....10.45 A. M.

...OMMODATION TRAIN.

...ilmington daily at...... 8.20 P. M.
...t Kingsville " .... 8.00 A. M.
...ingsville " .... 4.30 P. M.
...at Wilmington daily at.... 3.45 A. M.
...onnections made by both trains at Wil-
...with the Wilmington and Weldon Rail-
...Florence with the North Eastern Rail-
...Charleston, and at Kingsville with the
...arolina Railroad.

WM. McRAE,
General Superintendent.
336-tf

...NOTICE TO MERCHANTS.

...GULAR THROUGH FREIGHT TRAINS
...leave here on Mondays and Thursdays,
...rning, arrive on Tuesdays and Fridays.
...ons wishing to ship by said Trains will please
...their freight in warehouse by 11 A. M.,
...ednesdays and Saturdays.
WM. SMITH,
Master of Transportation.
...ov 1
333-tf

TRANSPORTATION OFFICE,
WILMINGTON, CHARLOTTE & R. R. Co.,
Wilmington, N. C. May 29, 1866.
...ROM AND AFTER JUNE 1st, 1866, the Mail
...Train on this road will leave Wilmington at
...o'clock, A. M., on Tuesdays, Thursdays and
...aturdays, and arrive at Sand Hill at 3 o'clock,
...M. Returning will leave Sand Hill at 7 o'clock,
...A. M., on Mondays, Wednesdays and Fridays,
...and arrive in Wilmington at 4 o'clock, P. M.
WM. H. ALLEN,
Master of Transportation.
may 31
203-tf

SUNDRIES.

2800 BARRELS FRESH LIME (two car-
goes) momentarily expected.
80 BARRELS HEAVY CITY MESS PORK.
1000 SACKS LIVERPOOL SACK SALT.
300 BALES PRIME HAY
100 BARRELS EXTRA SUPER FLOUR.
20 BAGS N. C. BUCKWHEAT FLOUR, pure

INSURANCE AGENCY.

We represent, in this city, the following Insurance Companies, viz :

THE SECURITY INSURANCE ...

...

ARE AS GOOD AS EVER.
Call on the Agent.
E. P. GEORGE.
No. 3 North Water Stre...
oct 12
316...

good on a plan I'd had to pick up the stuff that was out of place along the fence line, the beer bottles and golf balls and the bag of garbage by the gully already split to reveal a doll's head when I lifted it off the sodden ground. It felt like a bit of providence when the land also offered up a big black garbage bag, a smattering of holes like freckles, just a few things in it already.

I hadn't meant to look too closely. I didn't really want to know. But every so often I'd be putting in a plastic water bottle and I was pretty sure it was the breastplate of a turtle shell flashing back up at me. I guessed the whole thing was in there, judging by the bulge of the bag; I mean maybe not the whole turtle but at least the top and bottom of the shell, a pair of parentheses, still there.

I could not think of any explanation for this shell the size of a dinner plate taking up space in a Hefty bag. Or I could, but all of them were sad, and I couldn't see how getting a better look was going to help. By the time I'd finished that side of the property line, I had filled that bag plus another sack I'd found up there. I descended the bluff with the big bag over my shoulder like some kind of trash Santa, holding before me a two-by-three-foot piece of foam insulation that caught the wind like a sail. Where the trees grew close together, it pushed through the rasping cedar fingers like a shield, the foil side glinting merrily in my awkward grip as if an unwieldy sled was part of the haul.

I stuffed it all into a new garbage bag and took the lot of it straight to the can out past the city gate. I'd once left a bag in the holding bin next to the house and there were maggots on it when I tried to take it out to the gate, so I figured, Why not just finish it? Why wait for anything else to happen? So I drove it all right then the mile and a half down the sometimes paved road and eased it into the can that gets picked up every two weeks, and I was barely back to the house before I wondered if I had done the right thing.

So I ask Brian. It wouldn't have been right to dump the turtle shell out of the bag onto the bare ground, but taking it off the land didn't seem better. Maybe the turtle belonged here. Maybe it was kin of the one on the road that stopped the neighboring zoo director at the low-water crossing when she came out to visit. She'd texted a picture and the vet back at the rescue zoo had identified it before she even got to me waiting on the porch.

Maybe the trash bag turtle had been an exotic pet or the shell was just a souvenir, maybe it wasn't from around here at all, but what did that matter? I could afford to be wrong. There was certainly acreage enough. I'd always been glad for the occasional bone and feather and mollusk shell I came across. Surely, I could make room for this.

No one else had shared my concern. Not before I heard about Michael. Not after. But Brian figures why not go look. As long as we've been in the field setting things on fire, might as well round out what he calls our ten-year-old-boy-themed morning and go look at the remains of a dead animal. Brian was maybe concerned about the neighbors, about my being isolated out here, about how if something was amiss it was better to know.

I explain the geography of the trash barrel like an anatomy lesson, tell Brian where everything will be. Brian runs his knife down the skin of the plastic bag like a surgical incision. He is so gentle withdrawing the big glass bottles, the crushed blue cans, the wadded leaves wet and caked with dirt. If the shell had been intact on the mountain, it is broken now, the pieces of the top edged in a feathered jag like the way the bones of a skull knit together to form a vault. We see the lacework of a tiny bit of spine still attached inside the apex of that cathedral shell. I wonder which jostle against my own back might have broken it. Brian lifts on the blade what we reasonably believe is a mummified leg.

Brian is satisfied it might be sad, but it isn't nefarious. I can see some sense in at least keeping what was left together, even if that means leaving it in the split-open bag cradled in the trash can to be taken away. Brian says he is going to tell his wife about the bonfire. He isn't sure whether to mention the turtle.

Brian drives on home, and I look in on the ashes.

For days I go on watching the burn pit. I know how it can look cold but add one branch and a ribbon of smoke takes hold. I know how long it takes to catch, to rekindle, to die down, to snuff out. I know how you can throw in a bare trunk before you go, leave it like a nurse log so the coals will be banked when you come back.

I say cedar because everyone does, but technically it's juniper, has those dusty blue berries and everything. The cedar isn't exactly invasive. We're getting close to its upper range, but it's from around here; there just shouldn't be so much. All the cattle that used to come through mowed everything down and opened things up, and now that they're gone the cedar claimed it back before anything else had a chance. Endemic is what it is. A thing that had a chance to get out of hand.

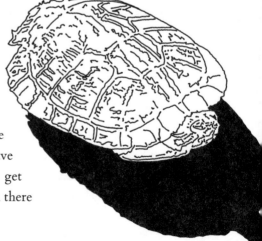

I don't mind feeding the fire enough to let it smolder. I don't give it too much fuel. I've got an eye on the forecast, and I pay attention to the wind. I remember I have other things to do—I get them done. But I'm down there burning the deadwood whenever I can. I've always liked math homework and doing the dishes: that category of clearly defined tasks you can become expert at, those uncommon spaces where you know when you are done and you can see the tidy wake of your labor. The burn pit is like that, except it can be hard to see absence for what it is.

Before the cedar choppers in these parts split the wood into fence posts, they used to burn it down to charcoal. Both charcoal and fence posts were worth good money, but the cedar choppers never got rich, spent their earnings like people who know nothing is going to last.

I don't know that anyone can tell the landscape has already shifted, that the sight lines are opening up again, that this part has happened under my hand. Mostly I'm the only one out here to notice. And anyway, there's still so much to do. It will take a stretch to catch up with fire to all that was brought down by drought. I'm not sure we should expect it will ever all get done. But flare by flare, all the cedar limbs that can be made to fit in the oval arena ring of the burn pit have now been fed to the fire.

I had some thought as I was doing it that I could maybe clear things for next time Brian comes out, make the next cuts easier at least. Brian was hired on when this sort of physical work was getting to be too much for Michael, and, one way or another, there will be plenty to keep Brian busy until it gets too much for him. Plus, now

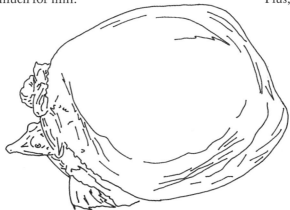

there's the rest of it, the stuff you can't saw and sweat your way through, that's on his shoulders too.

But in this window of quiet, while it's cool and damp and still enough, I don't have to wait on anyone. I have a fire to feed. I have more grief to burn. I can get the chainsaw back out of the shed and carry on breaking down and burning it, all by myself if need be.

By now I've walked away from the burn pit in every direction, spoked away towards the creek and towards the road and towards the house and towards the bluff. Come back and back and back. I've dragged boughs like sledges and shouldered others like bringing a Christmas tree home. I've held them aloft, one in each hand, like banners, like frightful wings, then let them burn. The sparks have climbed towards the stars. The ash has swirled down like a snow globe. Again and again, my face has glowed.

I have no idea what Michael wanted me to find in the house. I don't expect to know. But I've brought out of the thickets everything I could carry. I've moved enough cedar to give the oak groves room to breathe. I've carried out limb after limb, a ritual of repetition, my hands full and then empty. I've uncovered paths that were hidden, buried, overlooked. I clear the way, bit by bit, until I can follow them out.

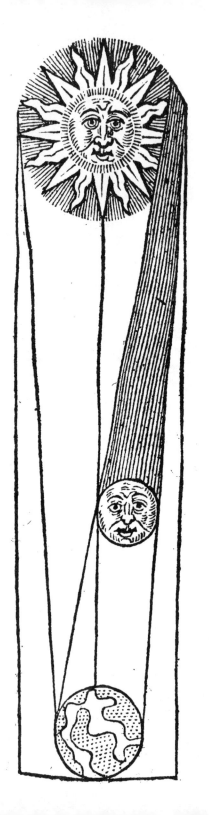
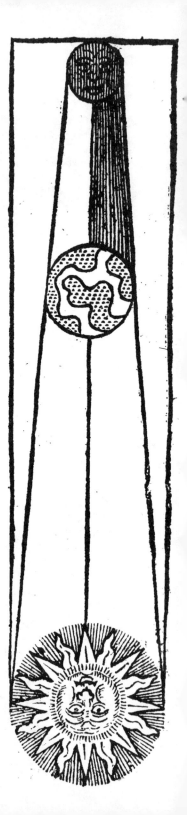

For we know in part and we prophesy in part . . .

—I CORINTHIANS 13:9

THE CALIFORNIAN QUAIL.

Ortyx Californica. Steph.

19

MY MOTHER GREETS
THE INANIMATE

"HELLO, MOUNTAINS!" MY MOTHER CALLS FROM THE driver's seat, cresting the hill, the Topa Topas that define this transverse valley suddenly on view as unobstructed panorama. We have not arrived during the few minutes of sunset's reflective glow we call "the pink moment." There is not that occasional dusting of snow that appears along the ridgeline when California somehow manages the twin feats of freezing and precipitation. No, there is nothing special except the fact of the mountains returned to our gaze, as they always are, from the top of the hill that takes us home.

My mother, as far as I know, has always done this. I don't remember it starting, and I don't remember it otherwise. Indeed,

I'm not sure I'd think to remark on it at all, would perhaps never have discerned it from the ether of family life, except that at some point my teenage brother, at a stage where one might feel a shock of embarrassment at basically anything parental, chose neither to ignore it nor to subdue it under the groan of "Oh, Mom!" It struck me even then as very mature, unexpectedly—almost subversively—generous, how he embraced the situation for its possibility, and responded.

"Hello, Bonnie!" the mountains now replied, the words slowed down, dropped into a deep and resonant register, as if reverberating from bedrock.

"Hello, clouds!"

"Hello, rocks!"

"Hello, lizard!"

Hello, Bonnie! echoed back in wisps and clatters and hiss.

If it hadn't registered before, it was now an event.

Sometimes it was just the acknowledgment of mutual salutation. Sometimes my mother had a follow-up remark or a question or a compliment to give, and the exchange might continue for another volley or two of pleasantries and observations before petering out, as greetings and small talk always do.

It went on this way for a while. But then my brother finished high school and left home, and I picked up the mantle.

"Hello, horses!" my mother would say.

"Hell-o-o-o-o, Bonnie!" they once again whinnied back.

Occasionally my mother would remark on their ability to throw their voices, almost like they were coming from inside the car. Sometimes she'd repeat herself to prompt them, should the initial greeting somehow go unanswered.

And there we were again, in conversation with fences and fields and creeks and quail and orchards and oak trees and ocean. Such good humor and grace: the whole world awake and available and condescending to speak our tongue.

And after a time, I, too, went away.

I called home regularly from my freshman dorm, asked how the empty nesters were doing. For a while there were stories about how my father had enrolled in flight school, how my mother had started teaching a class at the local college. The leaves had begun to crisp and turn outside my window. Then one day she didn't bother to mention their new adventures, didn't muster up any evidence it was all okay.

"Fine," my mother said, "we're fine. But nothing talks to me anymore."

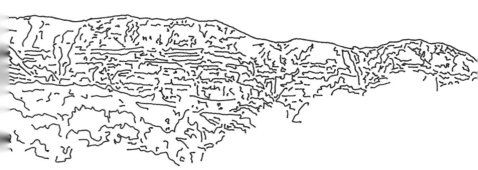

The bundle which he gathers is then held between what we have called the finger and thumb of the trunk, and is thus conveyed to the mouth : —

If the objects which he is collecting are too small to repay him for the trouble of carrying them to his mouth, he holds them one by one behind his thumb, till he has gathered enough for a load. Thus, if he finds a small root, he seldom eats it at once, but collects two or three, holding each in the following manner : —

When the object which he wants requires force for its removal, or is difficult to reach, he completely curls his trunk, thus —

20

CAPTIVATED

THE JARDÍN ZOOLÓGICO DE SANTIAGO SITS HALFWAY UP A hill. The llama pen looks out over the city's blanket of smog. The Virgin Mary, at the top of the hill, looks out over the llamas. The base of the hill is populated by pigeons missing feathers or feet, men selling foam lizards on wire leashes and rubber spiders that drop from your hand like a yo-yo. The hill itself, Cerro San Cristóbal, is steep enough to merit a funicular. The zoo is the only point midway, the only stop between the concession carts and the Virgin, the car and its counterweight pulling even as you step out onto the platform. The zoo attracts tourists and field trips and couples skipping school, and when a child calls out "Gorila!" there is no sign on the chain-link enclosure to say that the ape in question is actually a chimpanzee. Context is kept to a minimum. The zoo has no shortage of certain kinds of silence. It is full of half measures. It is an odd place to live, and it is a curious place to die.

I remember seeing pictures of New York's Bronx Zoo from the turn of the twentieth century: it was all iron bars and concrete, plain and easy to hose down, stark in the pictures as I imagine it was stark in real life. The pictures bore a striking resemblance to Chile's national zoo as I found it in 1998. Granted, there had been some progress, some innovation, a trickle of the enrichment programs popularized and implemented at other zoos around the world. The polar bears, for instance, had been given a plastic five-gallon bucket to bat around. And their food was frozen in blocks and hucked into the water at mealtimes so they'd have something to do, a puzzle to solve, at least for the ten or fifteen minutes until they shattered the ice and pawed out the fish. Ten or fifteen minutes, twice a day, is at least something. Otherwise, it was just the water and the bucket and the sloping concrete cage, all the same kind of cloudy white, all the same kind of blank.

Perhaps it is that hum of continuity, of things ever just like this, that means you can walk around in the tiger cages, with the tigers still in them. A visiting vet once reminded me to keep a wide berth if I decided to walk around the head of the anesthetized patient out cold at our feet. "You never know," he said, as we leaned on the cat and drew blood. "You can't be too careful."

But the zookeepers, the people who spent their whole day, every day, with the animals, the keepers taught me better. They said, "Eehhh." They said if you know what you're doing, especially if you've brought the tigers up from cubs, all you need is a garden hose, some running water, and your thumb over the nozzle. The tigers come too close, you give 'em a spritz.

"Don't tigers *like* water?" I asked. "Aren't they good swimmers or something?"

"They don't like the spritz," the tiger keeper said.

"Does it make them mad?" I asked. We were already inside the cage. We were already walking the concrete strip at the base of its grassy slope while a tiger paced a parallel track twenty yards uphill. My hands were empty. The zookeeper held the hose. I continued, "What if the spritz makes them mad?"

"Eehhh," said the keeper, spraying down the concrete as if it might bloom.

You can also walk around in lion cages, so long as you first put the lions themselves in an even smaller cage, the cell within a cell in the middle of their enclosure. Yes, flush them into that tiny metal box, pull the three metal panels in their tracks until they clang into place and cover the doors—then let yourself in and walk about as you please, carry on a conversation, toss bones long and thick as your forearm over the perimeter where you'll pick them up later.

Just, if you don't mind, try to speak up. Try to be heard over five lionesses beating against the metal doors. Try to forget that each door is just a single sheet of steel, the noise a *bang-bang-bang-bang-bang-bang-bang-bang-bang*, the beat of a boxer working a speed bag, paws hitting the metal panels as fast as if they were running, as if to get to you these lions would manage to sprint straight uphill.

There were other places in the zoo one might cheat death, but I was convinced these lions would kill you. On sight. For no other reason than the faint sound of your beating heart. I thought about this as I picked up a lion cub out of her crib in la sala de crianza. In English it translates to something like "intensive care unit," but in practice it was more of a limbo, a waiting room. It was home to creatures too fragile to be on display: the very young, the very old, and the very sick. Outcomes were predictable enough. Young things got stronger and moved out, old things lingered and stayed on, and sick things almost invariably died in the hours after we'd gone home.

The lion cub came to us when the mother wouldn't nurse her. The cub was the size of a puppy, except instead of feet too big for her body, it was the head she would need to grow into. Yet she had virtually no jaw strength. With a little help she'd get my fist in her mouth, do her best to gnaw on it, and after a while I'd pull my hand out again, unscathed and not even particularly damp.

Across the room, I wore a full chain-mail glove just to change the water dish of certain parrots. I still have the scar from trying to bottle-feed an enthusiastic baby boar. When a keeper offered to show me the proper technique for putting an arm into the mouth of a hippopotamus so that it won't be torn off, I listened carefully to how to steer clear of its rotating clamp—you go straight on, as if reaching for the uvula—but I declined the practice session. The hippopotamus looked less than game. I was learning enough as it was.

I learned, for instance, that the viscera of a Thomson's gazelle will splash out if you run a knife down its abdomen; that the first incision of an autopsy is like unzipping a piece of overstuffed luggage. Not that you'd set down a suitcase with its legs in the air, or have a duffel packed with viscera in the first place, every color of red and purple and gray spilling, pouring, washing across a metal tabletop without that girdle of abdominal muscle to hold it in. The vet I was with rummaged through the organs, poked at a bowel obstruction—the presumed cause of death—and then he cut the tube at the throat, the tube at the

anus, and pulled the whole vital mess into a bucket.

He made some notes. We hosed out the inside. We pulled the body down off the table, and I couldn't help but notice that the gazelle looked fine; the short white hair on its belly and between its legs stained a little pink from the blood, but fine. It was hollow now, but its shape hadn't changed at all. If you supported the head a little, it could still be made to stand.

I asked, "What are you going to do with it? What happens to it now?" The vet had curly hair and thick glasses that distorted his eyes, made them big and wobbly. He looked at me and held my gaze, then said something I hadn't expected. "Al museo."

The zoo, it turned out, had a museum. But since the museum was not directly related to my duties there, to the cages I cleaned or the fauna I fed or any of the sundry ways I assisted the vets when they called, I had managed to work a full two months at the zoo, without ever realizing there was a museum right in the middle of it.

Even once I'd discovered it, the museum still felt like a secret. It was secluded and cave-like. I could never remember its hours or how to get to it or the names of any of the gracious and hip twentysomethings who staffed it. Each time I wanted to return, it took no small amount of luck to find my way back. Outside, it was announced by the smallest of signs, and inside it was just a loop with low ceilings flanked by dioramas. For a few steps you were in the Arctic, then it was a savanna, the prairie, a rainforest, the jungle, a marsh—habitat after habitat elaborately painted and then textured with real sand or dried grasses or moss.

There wasn't a plaque or a memorial or anything to say so, but all the animals in the museum had died in the zoo. While the living animals of the zoo had enclosures of concrete and iron bars, the museum specimens were posed in painstaking reconstructions of their native habitats. Animals in the zoo were bored, prone to inactivity and nervous tics and self-destructive behavior. Animals in the museum seemed thoroughly engaged, stalking or leaping or flapping or grazing in blissful perpetuity. Their habitats were lush, and the animals seemed to thrive, though their glass eyes couldn't see the paradise. Their plastic tongues never tasted anything at all.

Inside the museum I thought about vessels and enclosures and tombs, about limbo, about the elaborate ways we send off the dead and the rewards we've heard might await us after a life of hardship and suffering and deprivation. What a curious inversion this museum was: the most authentic habitat in the whole zoo and it was available only to carcasses. And yet how familiar the promise: to have in death what they never had in life.

On my more generous days, I wondered if the zoo was, in a way, honest, stripped down to something irrefutable. Habitats are remarkably complex, after all, whole interlocking multispecies ecosystems, governed by more relationships than we can mimic. Any environment the zoo could mock up would be to some degree false, to some extent lacking. So they made no pretense of nature, no illusion of the wild. They had animals in cages and that was it. Just animals in cages. And some grass sometimes, a pool, maybe a tree if you were lucky, but a tree that grew in Chile, not wherever the gibbon climbing it would have come from.

I liked the phrase *jardín zoológico*, the way the word *garden* suggested both nature and its controlled, wholly unnatural cultivation. But then, the word was too pretty. It didn't address the brown bear kept in isolation behind the bodega, rescued from the circus, underweight, his fur worn away at the harness spots. It didn't explain the camel that foamed at the mouth, foamed like sudsy brushes at the car wash, sudden and thick and dripping the moment a visitor walked into its pen. It wasn't even rationale for the albino peacock, with its shivering tail of lace, sequestered from the others in its own concrete cage. No, *garden* was the wrong word. A bed of flowers never seems grotesque.

Biologists know better than anyone how quickly even the best taxonomies break down, categories ever imperfect, never a total fit between the fluid world and our structures to describe it. How alluring these systems of meaning and how inevitable their flaws. The medieval bestiaries are built on it, this yearning for sense and logic and rules, this looking at the world hoping to see through it. Many systems are total, but few are fail-safe. Very few things can stay contained. We must know: it is possible to escape.

At the zoo some creature or another slipped its bonds maybe once or twice a year. A tiger one time. A chimpanzee who roamed the zoo for hours before realizing his cagemate couldn't scale the wall to follow him, and so sat on the edge of the enclosure calling to her, singing for half an hour before he finally gave up and slid back down the embankment to be with her.

I don't remember if the flamingos had already made a run for it or if they were just inherently a flight risk. They didn't have a particularly sizable enclosure. Most of their space was overhead, just room enough for a short flight into a drape of netting, nothing big, but it worried the keepers, and the vets considered their options. They could sever a tendon and prevent that individual from extending its wing to fly, but sometimes the tendons grow back, mend, forgive the violence done to them, and the bird is restored to risk. They could instead just secure the cage, make it harder to get out, but ceilings, covers, overhangs of any stripe are thought to look bad. They draw attention to the cage. No, better to keep the cages open on top, preserve the illusion of freedom, of nature, and let the birds and their visitors see nothing but unfettered sky above the creatures born to climb it. Better to alter the bird than the environment was the judgment, borne out in a series of amputations removing part of the left wings. We did the amputation at the elbow: a snap, the nick of a scalpel, the whole flock done in an afternoon. We left a pile of half wings. I remember the shading of the feathers. And I remember the white dust of mites crawling out slowly, later, having realized the wing was dead.

In a place where I could traipse around tiger pens, pet bears through the bars on their cages, and choose between holding

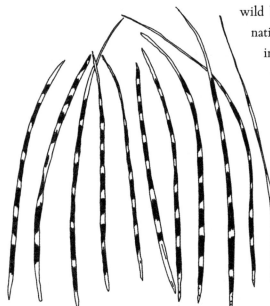

down the six-hundred-pound wild boars in need of vaccination or plunging a needle into all that hog flesh, the one area of the zoo where I was not allowed was with the elephants. Globally they cause more zookeeper deaths each year than any other animal. Elephants, the keepers said, are not suited for captivity. It makes them not mean exactly but something worse.

PORCUPINE.

The closest I came was trips to the vet, whose round office sat like a crow's nest over the embankment of the elephant pen. The path to the office door was narrow as a footbridge and reminded me of walking a plank. Sometimes the elephants wedged up under the railing, the ends of their trunks waving like sock puppets, gingerly feeling out what they couldn't see. Once, I reached out to the searching trunk and was startled that its skin was abrasive, rough like concrete and sprouting fine dark hairs that felt like wire bristles. The trunk reached in return, coiled in liquid movements around my wrist. They were the calculations of a constrictor and I could imagine the tug that would pull me over the railing, even as I jerked my hand up to my chest.

Even things you don't want you still sometimes have to keep. The last time an elephant died at the zoo, the staff had been not just relieved but downright happy. They felt good. They felt safer. They vowed never to get another and went home smiling. But what could they say when an ambassador read the sad news and sent them a new one? Sent them two, in fact. What could they do but order new feed and prepare to wait out, in fear, another sixty-year life?

It was no consolation to the elephant keepers that old age isn't especially natural. A swan in the wild, for instance, is lucky to make it past age seven, but protected they'll live more like twenty years. Some make it to fifty. It's as if, with enough control, enough care, in the right environment, a thing could last

LIONESS.

forever. Oh, the zoo had no short-age of neurotic parrots rubbing their feathers off or agitated chimpanzees plucking their shoulders bald. But if creatures can survive the stress of boredom, it's likely they'll live to endure it a very long time.

The keepers, when I knew them, were all middle-aged men. As a group they were what you might call hearty, strong if not necessarily in shape. They liked working with their hands. They were, as a group, fond of jokes and proud of their work and affectionate about their animals. Some kept small collections of feathers or whiskers or quills. They all liked working outside. They said they liked the freedom.

Keeping was passed down in families, father to son, men who hadn't in all cases finished high school hired into exotic animal care once their fathers retired or, as seemed more common, passed away. The job was routine, heavy, a steady schedule of cleanings and feedings and calling the vet when something looked off. Maybe, if the mother guanaco was suffering complications, you helped deliver her cria in the spring, but mostly you attended to the constant ritual cycles of food and water and waste. There were no interviews and no promotions. It was a job you kept until you couldn't do it anymore. There are things you hold on to as long as you can.

Me, I could watch. I could help. I could do the work, but I wasn't heir to a line. The zoo operated on a certain stasis, a promise of things always the same, always like this. Every day the guys in the bodega cut up the same kind of fish for the fish eaters, the same kind of meat for the meat eaters, the same four kinds of fruit for the fruit eaters, and then tossed the scrap into the same big heap. Every day the keepers scooped the food into buckets and fed their beasts. Every day there were some of us to scoop up the heap and haul it to the edge of the zoo.

The dumpster itself was standard issue. You see the same kind of big metal box at office buildings and apartment complexes and construction sites, usually full of plywood or garbage bags or thin plastic sacks of copier paper and coffee cups and spat-out gum. The zoo dumpster was notable both for its contents and its approach.

The wide dirt path starting from a Staff Only sign ran uphill past the toolsheds and the surgery and the chinchilla hutch until it came even with the dumpster's lip pushed up to meet it. The dusty dry path stopped an inch or two shy, leaving a thin gap where it suddenly dropped into a chasm, a pit, a trough. The dumpster was yet another enclosure, this one half-empty and half-full of feces, broken brooms, soiled wood chips, soggy newspapers, limp latex gloves, hypodermic needles splayed at all angles, a discreet scattering of flies, and all the peels and rinds and bones and scrap left over from feeding an ark.

There was also, as I looked in one day, one perfect white swan. Dead, sure, but perfect. No sign of trauma, no scent of decay, just the ivory mass of its body, the sinew loop of its neck. Swans are big, so big the crush of their beating wings can kill a man, and death does not diminish them.

You can't throw away a swan, I thought.

But, of course, you can.

There is always a vessel when you need it. And there is always another. Anything can be made to serve. You can fit so much into almost anything, pack it full of things it was or wasn't meant to hold. Everything that matters will be put somewhere, to be kept or studied or held. Indeed, the ways of holding nest:

the body of a swan held within a dumpster, the body of a gazelle borne by the operating room, all the other bodies ensconced in dioramas tucked away in a museum at the center of a garden halfway up a hill in the heart of a city sprawling towards the Pacific on one side and the Andes on the other. And maybe it will hold what you need forever. Or maybe, for all you can contain or channel or keep in place, sooner or later, some trace or some flood will be fugitive. Maybe that essential thing will be free, maybe held in something new.

There was a day I came down the hill and never went back up. I stopped to sing for no one, and the zoo goes on without me. The cages, in particular—the cages never change. The cages look the same for every species and the same from every side. The cages look the same to the sons as they did to the fathers, the same to this generation as they will to the next. The days count out years and the sons replace fathers and maybe it all goes on just as before, the vendors selling toys meant to be animals and the sculpture meant to invoke the Virgin high above it all. Or maybe, if I troubled to look back, there are new cages now.

HOAX

I WOULD HAVE SAID FOR A LONG TIME, I did say for a long time, that armadillos are born dead. I had no evidence of any other point on their life cycle, imagined them a sort of wildflower growing along certain depressing stretches of highway, not so much blooming as from inception already gone to seed. Like the Vegetable Lamb of Tartary, a creature sprouted from a plant, tethered by its umbilical stem and grazing—only even less likely. I have made concerted efforts to spot the triangular divots of their snuffling in the dirt, have searched very deliberately for their traces and bread-crumbs, and still I would have believed they were a hoax. Until one night in the new neighborhood. One and then two. Two and then four. Now we startle each other quite regularly. Now I am attuned. I have spent so long watching their cliff walking and stream fording and diligent searching and mad dashing that I know them by the sounds of their foraging in the undergrowth and can find them by ear. But still, it all happens not quite as often as I would like. And who knows how many I still miss?

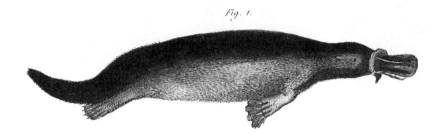

Fig. 1.

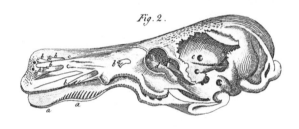

Fig. 2.

Fig. 3.

THE ONE

LINA AND I FIRST MET ON A BAKING SIDEWALK, ABOUT TO step into a car. It was August. She wore a black leather jacket and seemed to respond to the sun the way cats do to getting wet. She was dubious—of me, of the weather, of spending two hours in the car to witness twenty heats of an Iowa vs. Illinois tug-of-war spanning the Mississippi River. I remember her pressed into the corner of the back seat, pinned like a spiderweb.

Then my best field-tripping friend moved away, and Lina started saying she inherited me. We drove in Lina's car to zombie movies and crêperies, and we referred to the car by name: Señor Lobo. I never asked, but I feel confident the first name was Leonard. She wrote a book about myths retold, about la Llorona and Patasola and a musician meeting the devil at a crossroads. I drew the pictures: a butterfly, a cracked-shell turtle, a tapir so young it still had its spots.

Lina asked me to photograph her. Neither of us knew why writers had to be documented in images, why that was something anyone wanted to see, but editors and events kept asking and she needed a headshot she could live with. She came prepared with a black outfit, a gray outfit, and the skull of a jaguar her grandfather said he had captured, just brought to her from Colombia, her mother's light pencil script labeling the cranium's every bone.

Apophenia is a human tendency to see connections, to find patterns, though they aren't really there. Pareidolia is similar, the way we make pictures out of randomness, see shapes or faces, glimpse meaning where it doesn't actually exist. I find them both very endearing, how primed we are for recognition, for sense, for something to matter. How this finding is a kind of blindness and a kind of sight.

ONE TIME, LINA PICKED UP A RENTAL CAR AND DROVE FOUR hours straight to meet me in Minneapolis. Not just me, a whole gaggle of us, a motley and moving target inside the city unto itself which was the convention center. We counted it no small success when she found us. We'd unspooled text after text until she met us in the center of the maze. We felt confident that was it: the hard part was done.

Outside, the temperature was falling. The sun was getting low. The town none of us knew was becoming a new kind of unfamiliar. I walked with Lina to get her car, walked entirely through every level of a mostly empty parking garage as it dawned on us that she had spent four hours inside the rental car, within the belly of that beast, and in such a rush to get here that she had not stopped to clock what kind of car it was, had never registered how it looked from the outside. The fob had no helpful information. Any relevant details were on the paperwork locked in the car itself, with her luggage and her coat.

Nor did she actually know which parking garage it was. We did not have the name of a street. We had no make, no model, no color to look for, no license plate to hunt, no real certainty what the range was on the fob we kept clicking like bats, hoping something would honk or flash its lights. We walked with the fob alternately outstretched, like sweeping a metal detector, and pointed into the hollow of our open mouths—not even certain where one of us had heard that this amplified the signal, and definitely not sure if it was true.

Echidna of Greek myth lived alone in a cave. Half woman, half serpent, she's a mysterious figure. There's not consensus on who her parents were or who her offspring were, or even if her lower half ended in a snake tail or a snake head—or both, her torso emerging from the middle as if doing the splits. There's a lot we don't know. But she seems to be a mother of gatekeepers, sources connecting her not just to Cerberus, the three-headed hound guarding the underworld, but also to the redoubling Hydra and the secretive Sphinx.

Lina was pretty sure she was not parked on ground level, pretty sure it was not the top level exposed to the sky. Which left us an average of three levels it might be, multiplied by every garage downtown. We slowly learned that all parking garages look the same, skeletons both closed to the street and open to the weather. The wind cut through. It began to snow. Parts of our faces and fingers were going numb. The parking garages—all of them—were somehow colder than the now dark street.

A time-lapse montage of our searching would look like a still: one constant concrete vista, usually at a slant, a visual déjà vu though we had never seen that specific structure before and would not again, except we had both to circle up and then descend back through all these freezing rings of hell. We met neither Virgil nor Beatrice—we saw not one other soul—but eventually the echoing caverns of ever multiplying parking garages yielded an answer to the riddle of where Lina had parked.

We are not still cursed to wander the parking garages of downtown Minneapolis. We did not have to write off the car as a loss and explain to the rental car company lawyers that it was in a limbo of half somewhere and half disappeared from this earth. Yet I don't remember the moment of discovery. I don't remember the place or the relief. I don't recall any part of the finally finding it, the lightning strike of recognition after the long blank sea of same same same, of nothing clicking, of endless possibility, of no this isn't it.

We were grateful the car's heater was working, and we couldn't believe our good fortune that the exit ticket was waiting on the dash in plain sight. All that stood between us and dinner, us and completing our task, us and freedom, was the slim bar of a toll gate. The gatekeeping machine asked for the ticket and we fed it the ticket. The gatekeeping machine asked for payment and we looked at each other. We each had a credit card at the ready, but where to put it? We had already used the only slot to insert the ticket, and we could see nowhere else to put the card in this machine that had only one hole. Lina says in her head she was trying to translate *monotrema* when I blurted out loud, "Monotreme! It's a monotreme!"

EVOLUTION BRANCHES IN CLUSTERS CALLED RADIATIONS, and the living twig ends of the order Monotremata are the platypus and four species of spiny anteater, all only found in Australia and New Guinea. These famously egg-laying mammals hint at histories we don't really know, are both riddles and clues.

Early written records named one "duckmole" and the others "echidna," the whole lot summed up by the rather earthy "one hole" of monotreme. As if the triple threat of the cloaca was somehow more intriguing than the lack of nipples, the lack of teeth, the ears without protuberance to catch sound, the one-bone jaw, the spurs at the ankles at least originally venomous, the electroreceptors on bill or snout that sense presence and absence even when the creature is tunneled underground, in the kinds of conditions that make the stuff of this world hard, if not impossible, to see.

For who knows how long—hours, days, whole years of our lives—we could not distinguish one parking garage from another, one street from another, our car from any other vehicle, could find neither sense nor pattern as we bumbled along, but we knew, both of us, in a flash, a monotreme when we saw one.

A MONTH OR TWO BEFORE LINA AND I FIRST GOT INTO ANY car at all, I was walking on the rocky shore of a research island off the Great Barrier Reef. I was by myself, about as far as I could go, and suddenly there was an echidna coming straight at me. It

was the size of a box turtle, had a
similar determined tank waddle gait,
was of course armored in spiny quills. I did
not know then that these creatures are so strong they can cling
to a rock like a barnacle. I did not know they dig so adroitly in
soft ground, all four limbs spinning, that they submerge straight
down and disappear in seconds, if they want to.

I couldn't know Lina would come to text me "Do you need
this?" from every gas station and convenience store where she
discovers a giraffe pin or a sloth sticker or *T. rex* socks, whatever
token brings me to mind—the Americas apparently without
platypus drink coozies and echidna trucker's hats, or I'd know
about it by now. I could not foresee we'd spend years reading
the same one book with the snake on the cover, over the phone,
Lina sometimes hoarse from doing the voices, and that even
now I would find it the most reliable source of joy in my life.

On the island, I thought the echidna did not see me. I had no
idea that it was wired for a whole other kind of perception, had
access to a sense just for knowing if substance is or isn't there. I
might have been its singular destination. We'll never know. We
came so close. But I saw myself as an obstacle. I did my best to
get out of the way.

GIVEN

MY GODSON AT TWO AND A HALF SURELY DOES NOT REMEM-
ber me, having not been in a room together since he turned one,
back when his single word for everything was *light*. He surely does
not remember that I've held him, that there was a time he was smaller
than Iggy, their twenty-pound cat. He surely does not remember our
beginning, waiting with his mother to pick me up at baggage claim
late one night, that skeptical face babies have not learned to hide.

Yet when his father asks if they should prepare a gift for my visit,
he says yes.

His father asks, "What should we give her?"

This child says, "The moon."

And they do.

They blow up a gray balloon and draw on its craters and tell
me this story. And they give me the moon.

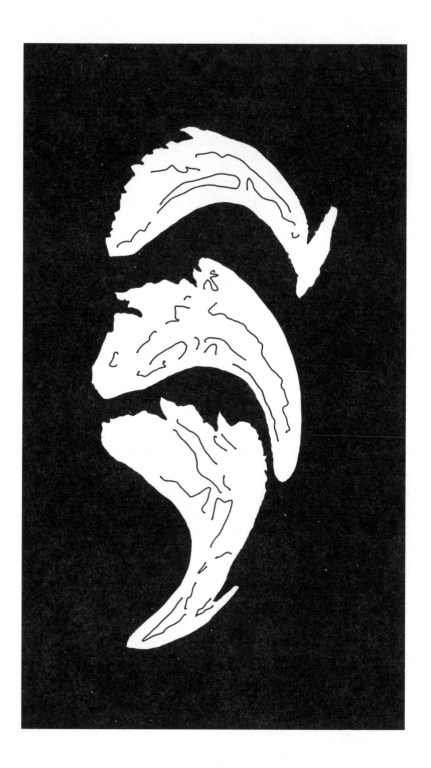

34

ON LETTING THE UNIVERSE IN

THE UNIVERSE HAS BEEN SEEN IN THE HALLWAY.

THE UNIVERSE DIPS IN ONE HOLE IN THE FENCE, THREADS A narrow space between, and reemerges from another. The Universe is marked, identified by scab and scar. I wonder if The Universe has been looking for a fight—if it has found one. I wonder if The Universe has been picking these fights, or if The Universe just keeps finishing them.

THE NEIGHBORS BEGIN TO LEAVE OUT OFFERINGS BY THEIR doormats. Vessels of water. Vessels of food. Then blankets and beds, a kind of vessel of their own. I leave the door open one day when I go to check the mail, and The Universe darts inside.

THE UNIVERSE ABHORS A VACUUM. ALSO A LEAF BLOWER. Sometimes a broom. The Universe loves the rug folded on the ottoman. And a chair with green velvet cushions I brought in off the curb. And the expanse of electric blanket across the bed, which, switched on, melts The Universe into a dark river, as much mountain as void.

WE DO NOT KNOW WHERE THE UNIVERSE GOES ALL DAY. OR why. We do not know what brings The Universe back. It seems enough to keep opening the door. It seems enough to release The Universe, when The Universe insists.

THE UNIVERSE SLOUGHS OFF GLITTERING MOONS FROM THE tips of its Universe toes. We find them scattered. We find more than we could have imagined once we know they are possible to find. The Universe leaves dead rats. The Universe brings in fleas, and for a month we set tea lights in little moats walled in shallow plastic lids. The fleas understand the heat as a body and leap toward it.

MY FRIENDS WANT TO KNOW ABOUT MY RELATIONSHIP WITH The Universe. Is The Universe mine? I don't mean to be evasive. I know I must sound like a cad. "I mean," I say, "we've been spending a lot of time together. Yeah, The Universe stays over most nights. Sure, I have a drawer just for The Universe's things. But The Universe comes and goes as The Universe pleases. We are both free agents. Why does it need a label? What do we ever own?"

MY FRIENDS POLITELY SEE IT OTHERWISE. MY FRIENDS SEE NO reason not to bell The Universe. My friends think I am honor bound to protect The Universe, and I agree, though my means are different from theirs. My friends are afraid I do not appreciate the responsibility, the obligation, the weight of what has happened.

THE UNIVERSE FITS BETWEEN MY THIGH AND THE ARMREST. The Universe curls over my feet and everything seems lucky and right. The Universe does not stir, and I wait in pain rather than disturb it.

FOR A LONG TIME THE UNIVERSE IS IRRITATED, CONSTANTLY, itching for relief until The Universe can't stand it. On impulse, recklessly or unthinkingly, The Universe rends itself once more. The Universe no longer scars. The Universe no longer scabs over and starts to heal. There isn't time. There is one wound after another. The cycle is picking up speed. From its beginning The Universe is an open wound, self-inflicted, cut again and again, no matter how we fret or scold, its rawness ever renewed.

THE UNIVERSE IS MYSTERIOUS. AND, WE BEGIN TO SUSPECT, expanding. I take The Universe to a specialist, and we learn more. The Universe is thought to be three years old. The Universe is known to weigh twelve pounds. It turns out The Universe hasn't been fighting at all. Or rather, it finally dawns on us, The Universe has been at war with itself.

I THINK OF THE ASTRONOMERS TRACKING HEAVENLY BODIES, the shapes they trace, the arcs and ellipses, the way a pattern starts to emerge and just when you think there is a phenomenon you can predict, it bends the other way, a physics you do not know.

THE UNIVERSE COMES TO ME ONE NIGHT AND SITS ON MY chest. The Universe does this sometimes. It is our habit, if The Universe seems amenable, that as I ready for sleep I invite The Universe closer. And though The Universe resists being held, The Universe can be met with one stroke after another, the contact always kinetic, until my moving arms, touching down like teeth on a gear, are around it, running down it, The Universe held in no one moment, but embraced.

IT IS MY FAVORITE THING FOR THE UNIVERSE TO DOZE OFF IN contentment like this: the head of The Universe at rest on top of my hand, my hand on top of my chest, everything stacked down to the earth and through it and back out the other side. There is nothing like feeling The Universe has chosen you. Even though you know you could be wrong.

A NEIGHBOR, TRUSTING ME TO SERVE AS MESSENGER, WAVES me over to her porch. My neighbor reaches into her pocket and pulls out a chicken heart. She says, "This is for The Universe." She says, "Take this to The Universe." She says, "May it please The Universe." And drops the heart into the cup of my hand.

THE UNIVERSE COMES TO ME ANOTHER NIGHT, TOWERING, stands on my chest. The electric blanket is bunched up beneath my chin like a collar. Like armor, I will later think. The Universe contracts. The Universe pulls into its density, concentrates its elements, and folds up like a sphinx. The Universe then unfurls. The Universe kneads and rumbles and brings its face close. The Universe leads with its mouth. My skin registers the surprising wet tip of its nose, just a speck of it, a cold and delicate glance, what printers mean by *kiss*.

THE UNIVERSE SUCKLES ALMOST AT MY LIPS. SWEETLY, YET
this tenderness framed every moment by the weight of
The Universe pressing hard. The Universe pinning me
at the throat. The electric blanket bent in a magnet's
arc over my windpipe, smothering taut, brutal,
the claws of The Universe flashing, close, not
quite cutting but nick pricking the air by
my ears, its intensity and its gentleness
impossibly immediate—the crush of
The Universe and the impulse that
I should endure it—all of it suspended and interminable, all
of it razor's edge, all of it
endless, all of it so very
nearly entirely too
much to bear.

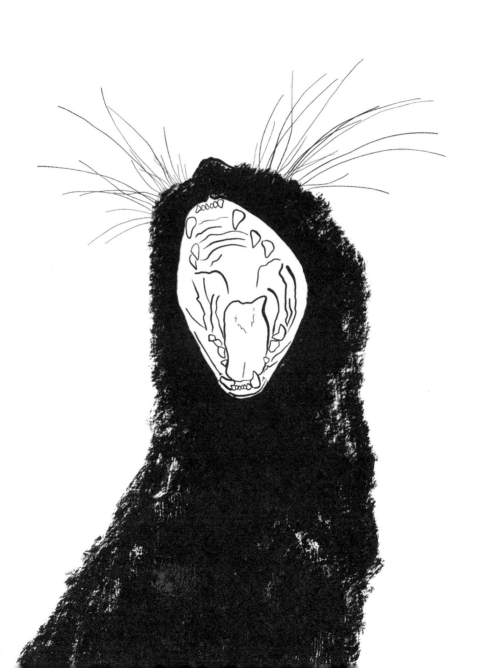

Sometimes I believe most in the imagination
for a long time and then,
without reasoning about it, turn to reality
and believe in that and that alone.

—WALLACE STEVENS

PEOPLE LIE TO GIRAFFE

It would take time, I suppose, for him to
get used to seeing higher things.
In the beginning, he might only trace the shadows.

—PLATO

GIRAFFE HAS SOMETHING STUCK IN ITS TEETH. A PEN MAYBE,
or a plastic fork. Giraffe perhaps would look impaled, speared
straight through the snoot, except the pencil is not yet sharp-
ened and it is at a jaunty angle and Giraffe has just asked without
any of the desperation of someone speared straight through the
snoot, "Is there something stuck in my teeth?"

Giraffe does not strictly speaking have teeth. Giraffe does
not have an alimentary canal, for that matter, and so presumably no reason to eat and chew and have particles wedge in
dentition or eddy up against the gums. Giraffe does not have
gums, come to think of it. Or taste buds or salivary glands.
And yet still Giraffe gets hungry. Still Giraffe is hoping that

everything tastes like acacia, perhaps your hair or your elbow or the cuff of your sleeve, might *omnomnom* it a moment just to be sure, longer if you shriek or protest and bat it away. Giraffe may slurp you with a big wipe of tongue up your cheek. It will make a sucking, slopping wet noise that you know is uncouth. Except Giraffe does not exactly have a tongue. Except that, by a different reckoning, Giraffe does. You tell Giraffe, by way of education, "We do not lick our friends."

|

ONCE I LIVED IN IOWA, WHERE I HAD A SIX-YEAR-OLD FRIEND. My six-year-old friend was the offspring of another friend, and I was standing on Church Street outside their house, and for some reason it was relevant to tell my six-year-old friend about the Santa Barbara Zoo giraffe.

The Santa Barbara Zoo has had any number of giraffes. The thirty-two accredited zoos in North America that have any Masai giraffes at all owe no small part of their number to one particularly prolific Santa Barbara Zoo giraffe, Michael, touted on their website as "the most genetically valuable male Masai giraffe any-where outside of Africa."

But Michael is not *the* Santa Barbara Zoo giraffe. Or at least there is a whole generation of us from a tri-county area that even now would know instantly if you said "the Santa Barbara Zoo giraffe" that you obviously meant Gemina— though hardly any of us would know her name.

In 2006, the *Santa Barbara News-Press* ran a story on the city's internationally known denizens, and it included Gemina, the only nonhuman among the likes of Nobel laureates and Monty Python cofounder

John Cleese and movie star Brad Pitt and need-I-say-more Oprah. If a certain level of celebrity is known by only one name, maybe the Santa Barbara Zoo giraffe was a step even beyond that, so famous she needed no name at all. It's rare stuff, but sometimes you have audience with such a creature, an individual so spectacular in her singularity she transcends one and becomes all, herself but something more, ascends not just to icon but ideal.

In 1826, Muhammad Ali Pasha sent a Sudanese giraffe as a diplomatic gift from Egypt to France. The next year he made the same gesture to regents in Vienna and London. Europe hadn't seen a giraffe since the Medici menagerie received a similar gift in 1487, the young female giraffe walking the streets of Florence, accepting apples from noblewomen reaching out their hands from upper story windows. The three nineteenth century arrivals captured the collective imagination, inspiring hairstyles and wallpaper patterns and the embellishments on crockery, of course countless paintings and etchings and woodcuts, but also dances and plays and cartoons and short stories, puffed sleeves tight at the elbow in honor of knobby knees, the perfume Esprit à la Girafe, and a color known as "belly of giraffe," not to mention a kind of latte art and the Viennese pastries Giraffeln and Giraffentorte, which you might still buy today and pop in your mouth. And they did all this—did more, in fact—while apparently hardly needing names at all.

The envoys to Vienna and London survived only a year or two, but the Parisian giraffe lived there eighteen years. Atir, the groom that stayed with her those decades, might have called her something, a sobriquet only they knew, but all that time she was known in the press as "le bel animal du roi," then "la belle Africaine," occasionally "the child of Egypt" or "Dame Giraffe" or "Her Highness." She is the source of the idiom "to comb the giraffe," meaning to busy yourself doing nothing, and it seems to have taken until Gabriel Darduad's 1985 book, *Un girafe pour le roi*, to call la girafe by an actual name: Zarafa.

I suspect I did not know Gemina's name even on the occasions I stood in front of her on field trips. I believe I've just learned it a moment ago, looking up "the Santa Barbara Zoo giraffe," the search results page one big chorus of "Gemina." I'm sure I did not know it when I lived in Iowa, not in that moment on Church Street, where maybe it was fall, probably it was dark but not late, likely we were walking back from somewhere and it was time to say goodbye, but for sure I was trying to explain the astonishing articulation of the Santa Barbara Zoo giraffe's incomparable neck.

"So . . ." I said, reaching my arm straight up, as if I were going to be called on, as if I had never been more sure of the answer. "If a typical giraffe is like this . . ." A regal posture of rectitude stretched through the limb, its line extended straight from the ground through the side body up to perked pointer and pinkie fingers, the middle and ring fingers closed flat to meet the pad of my thumb.

". . . then the Santa Barbara Zoo giraffe was like *this!*"

And as if what I'd said was *Timber!* the towering giraffe neck bent at the elbow and fell sharply to the side, the swift sweep of acute angle, a great hour hand thrown from twelve to two, then caught fast again.

"Note," I said with a flick of the wrist, "the head."

Instead of a faithful finial extending the skew neck, the head swiveled again as if to compensate, a commensurate angle, a second bend to return the chin parallel to the ground, ossicones alert.

Then, as if you can't stare someone straight in the face and say nothing, the mouth opened and greeted my six-year-old friend. And I discovered, to my surprise, there was now a Giraffe between us.

GIRAFFE CALLS BY GIRAFFONE. GIRAFFE TREMORS AN UPBEAT *brrrrrrRING!* and tips so the ossicones are angled like a handset waiting to be picked up.

Giraffe has a hit song. It's called "Pots and Pans," and it culminates with a raucous *DA da dada DA da dada bob bop BOP*, ossicones tapping out the last three beats on your arm or your nose or the top of your head.

If you tell Giraffe you have a surprise or a secret or some news or a gift—if you offer an apple or it's time to do the dishes or a swing on the playground just opened up—Giraffe will react with the same infectious, rising-pitch squeal, "Oh boy oh boy oh boy oh boy oh boy!"

Giraffe gets perturbed with a scrunch of the snoot and a stiffening of the jaw, and one ossicone starts to curl as the whole head trembles like the rattling lid of a pot boiling over. Giraffe gets perturbed sometimes for the sheer pleasure of it, the way one sometimes likes to sulk or pout or be disagreeable for a spell to try it on, but sometimes because it is the only proper response for not being taken seriously, for being dismissed, for being teased a little too long. Giraffe is so remarkably amiable—but surely that would perturb anyone.

Giraffe at peak Giraffe is an embodiment of attention, of wonder, and from that, joy. Giraffe is constantly thrilled—positively agape—and Giraffe also knows this is exactly how it is: everything a marvel. Every last thing.

‖‖

GEMINA—THERE WERE SIGNS BACK THEN TO SAY so—was fine. Her neck wasn't an injury. It didn't hurt. She was hampered somewhat in her peripheral vision, so the keepers fed her apart from the rest of her tower, but otherwise she was part of the corps. She was three when her neck first showed signs of eccentricity. No intervention returned it to orthodoxy, and she lived the rest of her long life that way.

Giraffe is older than my nieces, older than my godson, older than most of the children of my friends—certainly the kids I've known since they were born, since before they could speak, gripping ossicones tight in their infant fists. But it is thanks to these same children, and their years of study, that we know Giraffe development is a menagerie unto itself:

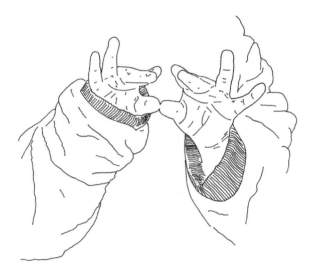

Baby Giraffes are born as snakes. The ossicones are still clamped to the snoot. The jaw is not yet hinged. They say nothing. Or they talk without moving their mouths.

As they mature, a tentative ossicone sprouts on one side of the head. The wandering ossicone may migrate to the other side, like the features of a flounder, like momentum conserved in a Newton's cradle, and it may at this time resemble a unicorn.

Or a narwhal. The second ossicone will likely develop alongside the first: the bunny stage. But even though it is a bunny, we all know it is still a baby Giraffe.

In some cases a third ossicone may present, the triple crown centered as a moose, or all to the side as a peacock, but soon enough the excess will reabsorb into the snoot. Baby Giraffes, like lambs and bear cubs, are most frequently born in pairs. The twins are mirror images except at times one more precocious, the first to pop both ossicones into place straddling the crown, while the other will lag a while longer as a bunny.

But eventually the baby Giraffe will be distinguished in its status only by being a little smaller than Giraffe, its voice a higher pitch. And that voice first and foremost raised to summon the attention and affection and company of other Giraffes.

|||

ALICE, JUST ABOUT TO TURN TWO, IS A CONSCIENTIOUS sharer. One raisin for Alice, one raisin for Giraffe. One bite of pancake for Alice, one bite of pancake for Giraffe. One Cheerio for Alice, one Cheerio for Giraffe.

Giraffe is a pleasure to feed. Giraffe works its muzzle and grinds its jaw and dip rolls like a wave in an elaborate chin-thrusting, glottis-bobbing swallow with a noise like *gulp*. Leave your drink unattended and Giraffe pulls at a straw or sips from your glass or throws back a cup clenched in its lips to the sound of *glug glug glug glug glug*! Giraffe is excited for you that there are leaves on your plate, even if they are not acacia leaves, which they almost never are but Giraffe seems undeterred. Vegetation of any kind is exciting. Giraffe will point out how lucky you are to have broccoli. Giraffe will nudge you a pea.

People will do things for Giraffe that they won't do for other people. Alice, for one, will not have a little more to eat, despite the exhortation of her parents. But she will have some more spoonfuls—or try something new or drink all her water or do any little favor, make some teensy leap of faith—for Giraffe.

Giraffe has unbounded enthusiasm for just about everything. Giraffe will tell you about ice skates and snorkel flippers and tap shoes and how to buy in bulk so there's enough for all the Giraffes and not just your own four hooves. With the same gusto, Giraffe will extol the virtues of the nap—Wouldn't that be just the thing right now? Giraffe may go lie down or just suddenly conk out and tip over. Either way Giraffe will snore loudly, baroquely, a long fricative snort on the inhale and a ridiculous *woo woo woo woo* on the breath out. Giraffe is trying to set a good example. You have to get your rest.

Oh, you may eat when Giraffe encourages you to—you may do all sorts of things for Giraffe's benefit or at Giraffe's request—but you will never consent to close your eyes.

Giraffe is trying to be a role model here. Giraffe is sure this is in your best interest, and really, Giraffe has never steered you wrong. But on this one matter you will never agree. Surely it isn't time to go to bed. Not now. Not yet. You aren't even tired. You have this waking moment; you will not settle for a dream.

||||

ONE NIGHT I AM AT A MURDER MYSTERY DINNER PARTY. THE tickets were a gift, and apparently when ordering there was a space to divulge some fact about the ticket holder. During the main course the cast works this information into the script, calling out three diners for questioning, implying their guilt.

I will not speculate why my gift giver chose to relay my connection to Giraffe, or why the theater company then chose to publicize it, but there I was, singled out as a suspect and this fact divulged. The detective was perhaps counting on flustering me, courting embarrassment, daring me to dissemble. I did not so much as blush. I have nothing to hide. I am happy to introduce Giraffe into evidence, certainly so, but I am going to ask the whole room to cooperate.

Oh, how game we can be! A hundred of us, strangers, have been together for maybe an hour, moving through this theater at the fairgrounds, and we really are all going to raise an arm in the air and hold our fingers just so and let a kaleidoscope of Giraffes falsetto shout in a windowless room, heads thrown back, "Hey-o!"

"Hey-o!" is a thing Giraffe says by way of greeting or when driving fast or while pushing someone in a shopping cart through the Costco parking lot at speed. It functions as preface or punctuation. It is an admission of joy and abandon.

I don't know if it's true—true that it happens or even true that anyone in law enforcement has ever claimed as much—but the actors who play cops on TV tell me it's the guilty who sleep soundly in their jail cells, so relieved are we to be caught.

ı|ı|ı

GIRAFFE LIKES TO ALERT YOU when there are Giraffes on a plane. This happens a lot, because a travel Giraffe can go anywhere. Reykjavík, Tokyo. Giraffe sends selfies from the Space Needle in Seattle, then the Harvard gates of Cambridge, Mass.

Alice, on the verge of three years old, has just picked up Giraffe from the airport. They

sit together in the back seat. The driver has not even gotten them out of tiny Burbank Airport when Alice has a wait-a-minute-I've-figured-it-out epiphany.

"You're a *talking* giraffe! That's *funny!*"

As if to say, "I *knew* there was something about you. Do you know what it is, old friend? Do you? You'll never guess! You've managed something that doesn't happen—and yet it explains everything. Can you believe it? How clever you are!"

Note she doesn't say *it's* a talking giraffe or *that's* a talking giraffe. She is not talking about the shtick or the fantasy or the

fiction or the puppetry or the hand performing it. The talking is a fact. The giraffe is a fact. The funny, for that matter, is a fact. She addresses Giraffe when she says this.

I know, because I am sitting there, too, in the back seat. And no one is talking to me.

SINCE THE DISCOVERY OF GIRAFFE, EVERY ONCE IN A WHILE a well-meaning relative sends a giraffe puppet. It's a sweet gesture. There are a few in the household now. I prefer the most diminutive: the finger puppets. I like the way Giraffe wears them on an ossicone, like the towers of bear fur donned as helmets outside Buckingham Palace or those extravagant Loyal Order of Water Buffaloes hats from *The Flintstones* or a wig fit for Marie Antoinette's court, all that yak and horse and human hair reborn as a teased-out pouf. If dressed at all, Giraffe is usually in mismatched doll clothes or the bespoke tissue-and-tape couture of Alice Designs, but Giraffe is just the sort of creature to appreciate a headpiece, to entertain protuberance coozies or sport ossicone enhancers with a flourish.

I recognize Giraffe's movements and expressions one evening watching Kermit the Frog—the pursing of the lips, the tossing back of the head, the way of dancing that is about leading from the body, head trailing—and wonder if there are only so many ways a human arm can be anything else. But if Giraffe is a species of puppet, what's remarkable about the giraffe puppets is just how starkly they bring into relief what Giraffe is. Giraffe is *so much better* than these mere giraffe puppets, lovingly sent to my door.

Maybe it is a matter of being unencumbered—the sheer expressiveness a tool as agile and deft as the hand can conjure—but still it shocks me: the illusion is so much better without adornment, without intercession, without the stiffness of cloth, without glass eyes or fake spots. What most needs representation is not color or texture or scale; it is the liveliness that matters. The essence is in posture, alignment, the minute shifts in coordinates by which one raises an eyebrow in challenge, drops the chin to show doubt, invokes both at once and dares us to bluff.

I think of the baby rhesus monkeys in cruel experiment who would tolerate a wire mommy that dispensed milk, but otherwise spent the day curled up in the cuddly folds of a terry cloth mommy. Except this seems like the reverse, the nakedly transparent thing enchanting us, become both nourishment and comfort.

｜ｌｉ｜ｌ｜ｉ

GIRAFFE DOES IMPRESSIONS.

"Do you watch movies? Do you know the movie *Star Wars*? Have you heard of it? Really? Okay, do you know the character Yoda? *Really?*"

Giraffe is excited.

"Oh, good! I have a Yoda impression."

Then Giraffe coughs and snoot scrunches and clears a very long throat. Giraffe shakes out the ossicones and turns away and then spins back, ossicones obtuse, an angle wide enough to evoke Yoda's pointy ears.

"Do or do not," Giraffe says. There is no try.

｜ｌｉ｜ｌ｜ｉ

IN MY MOST WIDE-EYED, WOO-WOO, EVANGELICAL, PULL-back-the-curtain-on-the-universe, if-you-are-paying-for-the-culmination-of-my-wisdom-then-listen-up professorial moments, I suggest to my students there are two core things human beings love.

We love confirmation—we love flow, we love belonging, we love being right, and we love a pattern we can predict. We love a thing we already know paid attention to, given a name, described and amplified and mirrored back. We want to be assured. We want the security of this is how it is. We need someone to stand witness with us.

And we also love novelty. We love the unique and unprecedented and maverick. We love firsts. We love upstarts. We love surprise and upset and redirect and change. We love shock and reveal and an idea so new, so totally alien, it fundamentally unsettles us, turns our world upside down and alters us forever.

That's it: two fundamental affinities. Old and new, connection and disruption, settled and unsettled. They are two ways of knowing. And we really, *really*, really love knowing.

I tell my students this is great news for them. Because chances are, as an artist or a maker or a thinker or a doer of any kind, you're trafficking in at least one. It's so very likely. You almost have to. You almost can't miss. Which should be an enormous relief, the very good chance you will, one way or another, whether you meant to or not, offer us some-thing we love.

And here's the kicker: you don't even have to pick. These two things we love, they aren't in opposition. It isn't either/or. There are beautiful strange moments that are *both*. At the very same time. You know them by the way they kick you in the chest, everything resonant and whole and shining, all at once, perfect, every bell ringing, yes.

ı|ı|ıı||

SOMETIMES I TELL MY STUDENTS ABOUT GIRAFFE. THERE IN the tower of higher education, I point out Giraffe is in an enviable position, comedically speaking. It is funny when Giraffe does things giraffes don't do. It is funny when Giraffe talks or pays taxes or offers to carpool. But then it is funny when Giraffe does a thing giraffes *do* do, like take a deep and abiding interest in acacia, because Giraffe has already challenged or subverted or upended our expectations of giraffes. You do and do not step into the same river twice. Giraffe is and is not a giraffe.

ı|ı|ıı|ıı

THERE IS A PARTICULAR PIECE OF typography, a kind of em dash doing a handstand, that I became quite taken by, found it elegant and useful and wanted a name for. It turns out it has many. It shows up in computer programming and mathematical expressions and downright rampantly as punctuation, goes by *pipe* or *bar* or the very word *or* itself. In Cyrillic script the little stick *palochka* tells you to make a normally voiceless consonant a throaty ejective, while the International Phonetic Alphabet claims it for the dental click. In Sanskrit it's a *danda*, in medieval European manuscripts a *virgula*, and in the notation of poetry a *caesura*: a whole family of notation for stop and pause and break.

But though it is capable of both sound and silence, wanders languages and disciplines—is suddenly everywhere—since 1913 it is known in logic as the *Sheffer stroke*. In that context it means something like "not both" or "not and," being without overlap or connection, like two parts of a Venn diagram that never touch. Indeed, what it means has its own name: NAND.

I have a nonbinary friend who finds this very beautiful, expansive. They almost gush, and when they do I see another reading of NAND. I had taken it as the limiting "not and" of only one or the other, but isn't there a way of thinking about it as rejecting the premise? That it's "not both" because it was never so limited to either/or in the first place? I had been looking just at the two Venn diagram circles, one or the other but never their overlap, but I'd overlooked all the infinite space beyond them, outside them, everything that is not in the circles at all.

I am glad to have found NAND. I like what my brain has to do to contemplate it. I attempt to bring it up in conversation for a month, but the finer points don't stick. I struggle to hold it as it is, not soften or simplify or metaphor it. But mostly my grappling makes me see how little use I have for "not and." It doesn't name a thing I need a word for.

What I need, what comes up constantly, what has devastating explanatory power that we ignore at our own peril, is something like BAND or maybe BOND: "both and." Here is complication and compassion and honesty and truth. And and and and and. Always another angle. Always another variable.

Always another truth. Improv figured this out a million years ago. Yes, and. Yes. And.

CORINNE AT AGE FOUR HAS ANNOUNCED THE EXISTENCE OF A two-headed fire-breathing Giraffe, "with two heads AND two bodies." Soon she has discovered a peacock Giraffe and an eyelash Giraffe and a big head Giraffe and no small number of species you would probably associate with draconic features or unicorn attributes but which she is sure are Giraffes.

Before she was even born, we had already identified the satellite-pinging space Giraffe and *wooOOOOooo*-voiced spooky Giraffe and the booming baritone of giant Mega Giraffe and confident if incorrect Super-Wrong-O and the rakishly misunderstood Giriffraff and the law-enforcement arm of Gira-five-oh, who will signal you with a whirring ossicone and a siren's *rrrRRRRRrrrrr* and then instruct you that—whatever you're being pulled over for, quite possibly "driving like a Giraffie"—the next time you do it, you need to shout "Hey-o!" and all will be right.

Yes, we know the rapid extension of ossicone exercises and the sudden palm-open pop of Mind Blown Giraffe and the awkward ossicone air quotes when Giraffe relays that the Italian editor is "wigging out." We know Nana Giraffe is bent and curled with arthritis, has almost an English accent but sometimes can't talk in more than a muffle because it's important to hold the steering wheel in her mouth and help Nana drive the car.

The Giraffes of some friends never speak at all, and others are furry in a way that makes them look an awful lot like llamas or alpacas, if you didn't know better. I sometimes refer to my brother's Giraffe as Golden Eye, for the glint of his wedding band, and it's Alice who was first to summon reinforcement with the twin calls "Hey, Giraffe!" and "Hey, Other Giraffe!" (sometimes, inexplicably, skipping over the OG as in Original Giraffe and going straight for the OG as in Other Giraffe). Across town my godson, at two and a half, looks at the dark crescents of his fingernails and announces loudly, happily, "I am a *dirty* Giraffe!"

I forget now whether I've told Porter and the nieces about the eight tiny giraffes or if I've only meant to. It's the only thing that seems relevant to add to their understanding of Santa Claus: that if you encountered something you'd never seen before, you might not know it was something totally new. You might, for instance, see eight tiny giraffes on a winter night, just a glimpse of them, maybe a whole long look, but if you didn't know there was any such thing as a giraffe, you might try to fit what you'd just experienced into a category you could grasp. We do it all the time. If you knew reindeer, for instance, you might use that word. And that's what it would be for you, even though it wouldn't stop being a giraffe.

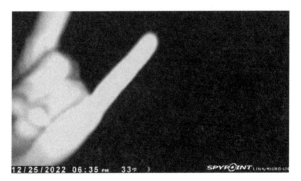

THE EARLIEST EUROPEAN REPORTS OF WHAT WAS ALMOST certainly a giraffe describe a hybrid: a creature born of a camel father and a leopard mother, the size of the former with the spots of the latter. The camelopard of medieval bestiaries lingers yet in the species name of *Giraffa camelopardalis*.

Meanwhile, it's only since 2016 that there's been any photographic record of the leucistic individuals known as "ghost giraffes." First it was Omo, a Masai giraffe in Tanzania, the next year a little family of reticulated giraffes in Kenya. They look like they've been whitewashed or dusted in flour, giraffes more primer than paint, except for the soft tissue, their eyes still dark. And just a few years after these first sightings, they are again apparitions, more story than giraffe. As with great auks and ivory-billeds, poachers reduced the mother and baby to skeletons, left the world with maybe only one known ghost giraffe. He's that mother's other child. He's since been fitted with a location tracker, attached to his ossicone, pinging hourly to affirm that the ghost, or at least the tracker, still exists.

If the old bestiaries are striking for their monsters and legends, surely more so, what should absolutely knock us flat, is the fact that we can trace nine entries out of ten to creatures that definitely exist. I mean, consider the whole process of reporting a bestiary, of gathering the science and travel journals and etymology and biblical scholarship from experts over centuries; remember all those manuscripts copied by hand, a scribe perhaps with the luxury of translating one page to a vellum blank but maybe working in mass production, several scribes taking dictation as someone read the source copy aloud to the whole scriptorium, their text introducing errors of the ear; imagine all this technology and scholarship, cutting-edge for its day, to render this artifact of an era both born of religious fervor and yielding the world's first encyclopedias—now stand in awe that all these games of telephone didn't introduce more inaccuracy than they did. At some point, harpies and phoenixes and barnacle geese only inspire the question: What doesn't exist in this world?

||||||||||||||

MEAN GIRAFFE IS A MYTH. THAT'S WHAT I TELL ALICE THE afternoon she wants to play Nice Giraffe, Mean Giraffe. Alice tells me Nice Giraffe is a girl and we like her and she is nice. Mean Giraffe is a boy and we don't like him because he steals Nice Giraffe's toys and takes them to a cave.

It's a solid narrative premise—characters! conflict! cave!— except for the casting of Giraffe. Giraffe does not envy. Giraffe does not dishonor others, and Giraffe keeps no record of wrongs. The more I hear about Nice Giraffe and Mean Giraffe, the more I'm inclined to rearticulate them as something like *Nice Things* Giraffe and *Arithmetic Mean* Giraffe: one not necessarily nice but afforded privilege and ease, the other not necessarily mean but behaving like most folks eventually would have to if deprived long enough.

"Why would Mean Giraffe steal toys?" I ask.

"Maybe," Alice considers, with that perfect seriousness of the very young. She hesitates, but sounds sure. "Maybe Mean Giraffe doesn't have any toys." I cannot tell if she is sad that there is a Giraffe without toys or disappointed that she has been denied the deliciousness of an enemy, the tempting line of category defining an us and a them.

"We could make some for him," Alice concedes. And with that, the ossicones twitch furiously *knit knit knit knit knit*, and new toys are made.

Handmade toys now stashed in the cave, Alice offers Nice Giraffe her toys back, but Nice Giraffe hasn't missed them. Nice Giraffe is happy to share. Nice Giraffe doesn't really believe in ownership and is not invested in material things. Nice Giraffe has been fine the whole time.

I worry that I am a bad aunt. I feel the way I do when Alice brings out her dolls and wants to play princesses and I talk in high-pitched voices about diplomacy and the struggles of being a regent and how complicated it is to manage a country, looking out for everyone's well-being without a representative democracy.

Which is to say I feel bad about not playing the game she wants to play. I feel bad that I am imposing a new narrative, when maybe the one she picked matters: maybe her vital project of making sense of the world benefits in these early days from this scaffolding of good and evil, nice and mean. I worry that maybe I'm skipping ahead, anxious to get straight to my precious truths about nuance and compassion and everything we can't know, that maybe I am rushing those gifts, no matter how honest they are.

I like to think when she grabs my forearms and swings two Giraffes into existence that she is not just invoking them or puppeting me, but inviting me to contribute, that this is how she calls me forth. But I'm not actually sure whose vessel she intends Giraffe to be. And I worry that by holding to Giraffe as an embodiment of generosity, I've set a limit, exercised control in a way that might be miserly.

Alice announces we are starting Nice Giraffe Club. Alice says that she is in it and I am in it and Nice Giraffe is in it, but Mean Giraffe is not. Then it is my turn and Nice Giraffe announces the one and only rule:

"First rule of Nice Giraffe Club: *everyone* is in Nice Giraffe Club!"

This is clearly not what Alice wanted. But she doesn't change the rules.

⁣ılı|ılı|ılı

WHEN ALICE IS TURNING EIGHT, SHE IS IN the grip of Carly Rae Jepsen's pop hit "Call Me Maybe." It was the song of the summer when Alice was born, and we show her videos of Jimmy Fallon and the Roots accompanying the artist on children's toy instruments. We show her Cookie Monster's parody, "Share It Maybe." We play the NPR version for the sheer pleasure of Scott Simon and Nina Totenberg being so whimsical and self-effacing. Family send her lip syncs. One aunt plays an instrumental version on trombone. Giraffe rewrites the whole thing as an ode to a girl and her Giraffe and makes a music video.

Before you came into my life, I ate acacia,
so much acacia,
so very many leaves.
Before you came into my life, it was all splendid,
and you should know that
it's even better now.

When Alice is eight and a half, her father invents Inner Monologue. It involves a funny voice and trying to voice what someone else, usually Alice, might be going through. Inner Monologue, as he explains it to me, is basically Giraffe but for the purpose of trying to articulate feelings and motivations, to see them and make sense of them. When Alice is on the verge of nine, I hit upon a similar strategy for saying what might otherwise go unsaid, what I call Psychic Aunt.

Alice has mixed feelings about Psychic Aunt, wants and doesn't want me to be reading her mind when I'm reading her face, her actions, our history, the room. But she experiences Inner Monologue as a total betrayal. She can't believe Inner Monologue is spilling all her secrets. No one is supposed to know her personal thoughts! Alice scowls at her father. Alice hates Inner Monologue. Alice still loves Giraffe.

ıllıllıllıllı

WHEN GIRAFFE ASKS, "IS THERE SOMETHING IN MY TEETH?" it is never so minor as a pepper flake, a smidge of acacia leaf. It is undeniable. And yet even a person who first admits, "Yes, Giraffe, there is something in your teeth," that same Samaritan will not continue to hold the line.

"Oh!" Giraffe says, spins and twirls and fiddles the object into a new arrangement. "Did I get it?"

And just like that, with the offer of a second chance, the truth gives way. At conferences and dinner parties and business lunches and pool parties, almost everyone lies to Giraffe—and they do so almost immediately.

"Yeah, you got it."

Giraffe is so relieved.

"Oh, thank you!" Giraffe says with the ballpoint pen still wiggling, dangling, bobbing up and down with those very words. What a good friend you are.

To be fair, no one answers such a question by reaching into someone else's mouth. No one just leans over to pluck the pencil away. This isn't a Gordian knot situation. We have boundaries. I mean, you would never: too intimate, possibly too unsanitary. Even when it's Giraffe. It just isn't done. So, the baton of a breadstick remains where it is, just swinging there, cantilevered out in the great wide open, the elephant tusk in the room. Maybe one is convinced nothing can be done, that the nicest thing in the circumstances is to lie. It's not like Giraffe is going to a job interview. It's fine. Don't worry about it, Giraffe.

Yet I think it goes both ways. We lie to Giraffe because it tacitly does not matter. Giraffe is not real. Giraffe's teeth are not real. The thing stuck in Giraffe's teeth *is* real, but it's probably not edible and it isn't actually stuck. So what does it matter? Giraffe isn't trying to impress anyone. This isn't a first date. Sure, Giraffe, it's fine.

And, I think, we also lie to Giraffe because it *does* matter. Something matters. You can tell, I think, because we aren't just denying or dismissing, we're mirroring. We meet this playful act with play. We meet this funny question with a joke of our own. We see absurdity and raise it one. Giraffe may be a fleeting incarnation, but we can still josh and rib and tease. Which

means this lie is also an affirmation. You don't lie to something that isn't there.

It shocked me at first, the bald mendacity, how quickly it was reached and how acceptable it was. It was close to a given. Only my friend the improv actor solved the loop of "Did I get it now?" holding up her phone like a looking glass. Here, Giraffe, this is how it is. Otherwise, it might as well be axiom: we lie to Giraffe. Almost without exception, and almost as soon as we can. It was disheartening at first. And then, it was kind of beautiful.

THE DALLAS MUSEUM OF ART ONCE INSTALLED THE JOHN Biggers painting *Starry Crown*. In it, three figures modeled on women from the artist's family sew, patterns of African and American origin woven around them, a red thread linking their mouths and their work. The museum asked visitors to reflect on wisdom from an important woman in their lives, and I spent a year making sense of the fourteen thousand responses they returned, handwritten in graphite on gray and fawn-colored paper squares.

It was a lot to take in, so I made categories. There was wisdom about food, animals, beauty, self-worth, money, jobs, relationships. There were famous quotes and song lyrics and something I came to call "true because it rhymes." There were stacks of do and don't, always and never. Beyoncé was a category unto herself.

Eventually I arrived at a seventy-one-point taxonomy to organize the glut of wisdom. And for all that reading, all that categorizing, all that considering, I remember almost none of the specific adages and advice. I remember the vast repetition of "This too shall pass," more common than anything else, and I remember the singular alert, "Don't look now: there's a spooky skelly inside you!"

But seeing it all, en masse, I came to hold a truth I now see everywhere. Ultimately, at its core, wisdom boiled down to a matter of declaratives and directives. As if the world were either substance or motion, observation or analysis, product or process, static or active, immutable or transient, noun or verb, body or soul. There seemed to be only two things we need to know, maybe only two things we can even hope to know: how it is and what to do about it. Either one might save you.

And note: not uncommonly, they arrive as a pair.

⫿⫿⫿⫿⫿⫿⫿⫿

ALICE, AT CERTAIN POINTS IN HER SCRUTINY OF WHAT WE tell her about the world, has asked both "Is that true?" and "Are you fibbing?" Honestly, the answer to either is usually yes. Yes, giraffes have purple-black tongues that protect them from the sun. Yes, your hair tastes like acacia. Yes, they are born as tall as your daddy, and in that birth fall the same height to the ground. Yes, there is a big blue ball that rolls down city streets getting bigger and it might be following you. Yes, okapis appear to be wearing zebra pants and have ossicones too. Yes, the problem with the plumbing is another case of pipe giraffes. Yes, I'll still be here when you wake up.

If the world were a binary of true and untrue, real and unreal, is and isn't, you wouldn't actually need two questions. You could get by with one and deduce the rest. But note there are two questions. Note how these two could-be synonymous queries aren't the same at all: truth being about the state of things and fibbing being an act with an agent. The way truth can be bitter, but we are fed and will swallow a lie. As if truths just simply are—revealed or found or hard-won, perhaps, but in essence already there—while fibs must be fashioned, brought into being.

We have a lot of words to certify what is. Just in English, we have *fact* and *truth* and *real*, *accuracy* and *veracity* and *actuality* and *materiality* and *verity* and *sooth*. But we have perhaps even more words to shade what isn't. Whether *illusion* or *pretense*, be it *imagined* or *feigned* or *concocted*, we don't just *lie* but *dissemble*, *prevaricate*, *equivocate*, *palter*. We spin *yarns* and trade *whoppers* and tell *fish stories*. We fabricate *falsehoods* and *fantasies* and *fairy tales*.

Fiction comes from the Middle English *ficcioun*, an invention of the mind, borrowed from Middle French, borrowed from Latin, made from *fiction* or *fictio*, an action: to mold, to fashion,

to make a likeness. I've always liked that, *fiction* a thing that is made, much the way I like how *essay* can mean to attempt.

It matters, I think, where fiction is a matter of likeness and essay is a matter of trying. So often we talk as though the truth you discover, and a lie you invent. But always that stark simplicity fails us, isn't enough. Both the journalist and the novelist write a *story*. Meaning can be made or found. And just ask Pinocchio or the Velveteen Rabbit: even *real* is a thing you can become.

UNTIL ALICE STARTED ASKING, *FIBBING* WAS NOT A THING I had thought about, not even a word I had used, for decades. It is a childish word, pertains to a certain relationship with the world where the rules of what is and isn't, can and can't be, are notably fluid, porous, flexible, and uncertain. Imagine what all it must mean: we have a word for not just a trivial lie, but a childish one.

I love how the word *fibbing* bubbles from Alice's childish lips, the way it manages both effervescence and gravitas. It's such a nice word, *fib*, funny and old and specific. Like so many words, like *yield* and *stop*, it contains both a noun and a verb. The noun has been fixed for some time, used at least since 1611 the way we use it now. The verb, however, has shape-shifted a bit since it first meant "to pummel." Maybe there's some root physicality in *fib*, the same shaking up we see in *josh* or *tease* or a literal poke in the ribs, that unsteadying collision that signals meaning won't come at face value. We don't know where that beating sense of *fib* comes from, don't know the heart or wellspring of the verb, but there is some reason to think the noun may come down to us from *fable*.

If to fib is to fable, to tell a symbolic story, and quite possibly one involving an animal, to enlist the remarkable to impart some moral or better yet some truth, then I recognize myself not just as a fibber but a fabulist. Which, obviously, is fabulous. Indeed, fantastic! Incredible! Almost unbelievably so. I am very conscious that I do not want to lie to Alice, but I am happy to fib. I will offer up every species of joy and jostle and illumination and curious possibility I know. I will try to connect. And if she needs more than the patent absurdity or sheer unlikeliness, more than my wink or my tone or my eyebrows raised just so, if she needs my worldly experience to supplement hers and has to ask, "Are you fibbing?" I am delighted to confirm that I am.

ılıl|ılı|ılıl|ılıl|ıl

GIRAFFE IS ALWAYS SORRY TO LEAVE YOU—GIRAFFE HAS been having a marvelous time—but Giraffe won't go before initiating the Long Giraffe Goodbye. Giraffe calls for all the Giraffes present. Giraffe waits for them to appear and circle up. Giraffe does not mind one bit that some of the manifest look doubtful.

"Byeeee!" Giraffe will wave, with a swift metronome sway of the head. The other Giraffes, a few reluctantly, ape along. "Later!" Giraffe arcs the greeting like a rainbow, and the chorus of Giraffes echo with only a tiny delay. "Ciao!" Giraffe leads with the cheek to pull a long horizon line, and the counterparts follow. "Bless bless!" Giraffe flicks left and right, rippled by the circle. "Moikka!" Giraffe bobs forward, and the assembled mirror back.

If you know *aloha* or *namaste* or *sayonara* or *adios* or *kia ora* or *zai jian* or *annyeong* or *paalam* or *auf weidersehen* or *uz redzēšanos* or *ma'a as-salama* or *dasvidaniya* or *arrivederci* or *güle güle* or *pip pip* or *tchau tchau* or *hoo roo* or *wodderyereckon* or *au revoir*, Giraffe will find its motion and loop it in. The goodbye only gets longer. It needs enough pieces to be whole. It has to endure long enough to matter, to mean something, to resolve into something else. There are things that can do this: both cast and break a spell. It stalls the parting, a thing we only talk about, until it makes it true.

ılıl|ılılılılılıl|

COSMIC UNCONSCIOUS
COSMIC SPACE
HIERARCHICAL STRUCTURE OF THE BRAIN
LINK BETWEEN PSYCHE AND MATTER
OBJECTIVE COLLECTIVE UNCONSCIOUS
'MOLECOLOGICAL' SPACE
PSYCHIC ENERGY-FORM DIAGRAMS
JUNG
MANDALAS
ARCHETYPAL IMAGES
SUBJECTIVE COLLECTIVE UNCONSCIOUS
'STREAMSCAPE'
MYTHS
FREUD
ARCHETYPES
ANIMAL SPACE
DARWIN
GOETHE
FISH SPACE
AMPHIBIANS
MECHANICAL SPACE
STREAMLINED SPACE
TELEGRAPH
TELEPHONE
ELECTRIC LIGHT
ELECTRONIC SPACE
T.V. RADAR
COMPUTER
EINSTEIN
COSMIC SPACE
URBAN SPACE
SUBJECTIVE COLLECTIVE SPACE
'MEGALOPOLIS'
OBJECTIVE COLLECTIVE SPACE
ECOLOGY
'SPACESHIP EARTH'
COSMIC SPACE

Fig. 4.   Tongue of the Octopus (*O. vulgaris*).
Magnified 12 diameters.

ACKNOWLEDGMENTS/CREDITS/CREDO

THIS IS A BOOK OF ARTICULATION: OF LANGUAGE AND VISION, and bringing together. I have never been so awake to the fact that who I am, how I think, what I know is assembled from moments and facts and fragments of conversation, so so so very many of them, in such a lot of places over so much time, but just staggeringly: in relationship with so very many beings. I am humbled, and grateful, and broken open by it. Any cataloguing or taxonomy of it is daunting, indeed impossible, but let me begin to describe this beast.

I am indebted to the old bestiaries, the minds and hands that informed them, the institutions and individuals who have kept or made them available long enough for me to know. My touchstones include the University of Aberdeen's 12th century Manuscript 24, the works in The Getty Museum's 2019 exhibition and subsequent *Book of Beasts: The Bestiary in the Medieval World* edited by Elizabeth Morrison, Richard Barber's *Bestiary: Being an English Version of the Bodleian Library, Oxford, MS Bodley 764*, and T. H. White's *The Bestiary* collection at the Harry Ransom Center.

Florence Fearrington's collection of rare books on cabinets of curiosity, natural history, taxidermy, and children's books featuring animals—and my access to it as a Marjorie Bond Research Fellow at UNC's Wilson Library—grounded me in the bestiary's legacy, made me audibly gasp in special collections, repeatedly, sometimes shriek with joy. Adaptations of photographs from my encounters with those pages bear witness in this book, including the artistry within:

》→ *The Philosophical Grammar; Being a View of the Present State of Experimented Physiology, or Natural Philosophy* (c. 1762)

》→ *Bertruch's Bilderbuch für Kinder* (1824)

》→ *The Sacred Theory of the Earth: Containing an Account of the Original of the Earth, and of all the General Changes Which it hath already undergone, or is to undergo, Till the Consummation of all Things* (1690)

》→ *Leonardi Plukentii, M.D. Opera Omnia Botanica* (c. 1690)

》→ *Testacea Musei Caesarei Vindobonesis* (1780)

》→ *Museum Metallicum* (1648)

》→ *The Wonders of The Great Deep; or the physical, animal, geological and vegetable curiosities of the ocean, with an account of submarine explorations beneath the sea, diving, ocean telegraphing, etc.* (1874)

》→ *Rerum Naturalium Historia* (1773)

》→ *Le Jardin, et Cabinet Poétique de Paul contant apoticaire de poictiers* (1609)

》→ *Rariora naturæ & artis, item in re medica, oder, Seltenheiten der Natur und Kunst des Kundmannischen Naturalien-Cabinets, wie auch in der Artzeney-Wissenschaft* (1737)

》→ *La Ménagerie Impériale* (1812)

》→ *Curiosities in the Tower of London Vol. I.* (1741)

》→ *Descriptive and Pictorial Sketches of the Animals and Birds contained in Forepaugh's Menagerie. Compiled from the Best Authorities. Designed for the Instruction and Assistance of Those Who Delight in Natural History* (1870)

≫→ *Alle de Ontleed- Genees- en Heelkundige Werken van Fredrik Ruysch* (1744)

≫→ *Museum Leverianum, containing select specimens from the Museum of the late Sir Ashton Lever, Kt. With descriptions in Latin and English* (1792)

≫→ *Observations, Naturall and Morall. With a Short Treates of the Numbers, Weights, and Measures, used by the Hebrews; with the valuation of them according to the Measures of the Greeks and Romans* (1636)

≫→ *Jardin des plantes en estampes, dessiné et lithographié par A. Adam* (c. 1865)

≫→ *Museum d'Histoire naturelle, Paris. Guide des étrangers au Muséum d'Histoire naturelle* (1828)

≫→ *Catalogue or guide book of Barnum's American Museum, New York: Containing descriptions and illustrations of the various wonders and curiosities of this immense establishment, which have been collected during the last half century from every quarter of the globe.* (c. 1862)

≫→ *Illustrated and Descriptive History of the Animals contained in Van Amburgh & Co's New Great Golden Menagerie* (1880)

≫→ *La Ménagerie Imperiale* (1812)

≫→ *Verzeichniss sämmtlicher in der grossen menagerie von Chr. Renz befindlichen thiere, nebst einer kurzen beschreibung der merkwürdigeren und ihrer lebensweise.* (c. 1860)

≫→ *Jardin Des Plantes: La Ménagerie et la Vallée Suisse en estampes* (c. 1854)

≫→ *Aquarium Notes: The Octopus; or, The "Devil-Fish" of Fiction and of Fact* (1875)

SPECIAL THANKS TO MY LIBRARIANS AT UNC CHAPEL HILL; Aaron Smithers, Emily Kader, Sarah Hoover, and Josh Hockensmith in particular. Alan Weakley gave an eye-opening tour of the herbarium.

Images also in conversation include *The Birds of America* (1942), photo negatives from Louise M. Perry, my own mammography film, the motion sensor capture of the Paisano game cam, and botanical monoprints made with the extraordinary Dan & Rebecca Collins. My drawing of lab mice is inspired by a photograph by Adam Gault, and the spiny softshell turtle by one from Patti Clark. I started drawing wasps from Joe Wilson's documentation and finished from my own observations in a gazebo and outside the Baldwin Library.

Ali Beyer, Audrey Niffenegger, and Stephen DeSantis put me in the path of book arts. The UICB's Penny McKean gave me the language of materials testing and Sarah Langworthy gave me an assignment that changed my life. Editor Erica Mena taught me my books could be anything I imagined—if I could figure out how to get it done. I will forever be thankful John Siciliano took note of a strand of seaweed, and told me to draw.

A version of "Wild Chilean Baby Pears" appeared in *The Normal School* and "Captivated" in *Drunken Boat*. Both "*Megalonyx jeffersonii*" and "Speaking of Basheis" were published in *Freeman's* (the Animals and Conclusions issues, respectively); and they had been previously incarnated as letterpress objects and artists books, as were "Love is in the Airport," "Intelligent Design," and "Captivated." Stephen J. West is adapting a spindle book version of "Flip."

This book was outlined as a project at Willapa Bay AiR (where I saw no less than four bears), and brought to fruition with additional support at Soaring Gardens (where I crossed paths with a very large cub), VCCA (where a fox ran past my studio), Yaddo (where I learned groundhogs can climb trees), MacDowell (ditto porcupines), Wildacres (where the turkey and I walked parallel paths), and MacDowell again (where just the photo of a monkey slug caterpillar kindled a friendship). The Fulbright program and Jacob K. Javits Fellowship contributed at the earliest stages to what would become this book. The singular legacy of the Dobie Paisano ranch and the Ralph A. Johnston Memorial Fellowship that made it possible for me to inhabit its acreage—with the profound care of Michael Adams and Brian Van Reet—ushered me through much of the later ones.

Most of these essays first met the world in readings. Some public, like the Anthology reading series under the helm of Cutter and Jeff, or Sanderia Faye's LitNight, but mostly more intimately, in front of fireplaces, on back porches, among the antiquities of actual parlors, in kayaks in the middle of a creek. They have traveled as phone calls from my writing desks in Iowa City and Dallas and Austin and Peterborough, been encircled by students at the arboretum, and told to astronomers in the Great Smoky Mountains on a starless night. They have been read by headlamp under the arches of an old stone chapel and illuminated larger than life within an amphitheater covered in moss, under a crisp and twinkly sky.

The great friends of these essays include John Freeman, who also invented a dog; Alice and Corinne, who have asked for them as bedtime stories the last two years at least; their witness of and with these essays rivaled only by the endlessly generous, incomparable Lisa Huffaker.

There are no better champions for my curiosity than my agent, Duvall Osteen, and editor, Masie Cochran: Best. The whole Tin House team should be crowned in laurels, including my bewitching pen pals, the always deft and savvy and humorous and humane Nanci McCloskey, Becky Kraemer, Jacqui

Reiko Teruya, Jae Nichelle, Justine Payton, Elizabeth DeMeo, Alyssa Ogi, and Isabel Lemus Kristensen. Anne Horowitz's scrupulous copy edits introduced the first known appearance of "Deadline Giraffe," and Dassi Zeidel's proofreading queries provoked a most rewarding fact checking among the Balloominati. Holy cow, Beth Steidle—I am astonished to be in any way collaborating with you and, truth be told, continue to live in awe.

Of course the work springs from the company of writers and artists and thinkers of all stripes, seen and unseen on these pages. I am grateful to the letters, essays, stories, poems, and prefaces that seed the epigraphs. Likewise to early readers Jess Wilson, Kisha Lewellyn Schlegel, Lina Ferreira, Sarah Viren, Amy Leach, Elena Passarello, and Ben Fountain. The wit and insight of my dearest family and friends and friends' families ring from these sentences—including Ellen Richardson, Jill Walton, Earl Zaromb, Lee Marchalonis, Toni Jensen, Tim Coursey, Fowzia Karimi, the Sharp family, and the Pelster-Wiebes—truly, you are innumerable, and I hope you each know that I know exactly who you are.

I carry Sigurður Atlason, Billie and Wallace Crosby, Thad Engling, Jackie Wiebe, and Joseph Yeh, always, because of things they once said to me. Jabe Bortolussi was the first person I knew to re-limb action figures. Janet "Sparky" McCracken understood early what both philosophy and studying abroad would mean to me. Jennifer O'Brien let a sophomore into The Psychology of Language. Corinne Rose posed a question I then put to others. Buster Balloon first developed the invisible T. rex eating the slowest caveman in the world. Ellie and Jasper, thank you for taking Giraffe to tae kwon do. Tinna, take your time, but I still mean it: You get to pick the next book.

I cannot name the strangers, or very many of the creatures, but they matter no less for that.

A. Kendra Greene

is the author and illustrator of *The Museum of Whales You Will Never See*. At eighteen, she interned at Chile's national zoo because there was no more sensible place to send a philosophy major. She became an essayist during a Fulbright in South Korea while she was supposed to be making photographs. She has an MFA in nonfiction and a graduate certificate in book arts from the University of Iowa, where she was both a Jacob K. Javits fellow and costumer to a giant ground sloth. She's been the writer in residence at the Dallas Museum of Art, and longtime guest artist at the Nasher Sculpture Center. Her work has been supported by fellowships from MacDowell, Yaddo, the American Library in Paris, and Harvard's Library Innovation Lab. She has lent her voice to audiobooks, radio broadcasts, and anime Amazons. Briefly a high school math and science teacher, she has since taught creative writing, with a bent for text and image and object, at the University of Iceland, UNC Chapel Hill, and UT Dallas. She finished this book after a season on the historic Dobie Paisano Ranch, surrounded in equal measure by critters and the sheer mythos of Texas, which is to say, close enough to the lions of the Austin Zoo to hear them at twilight, roaring or talking or yawning, depending on who you ask.

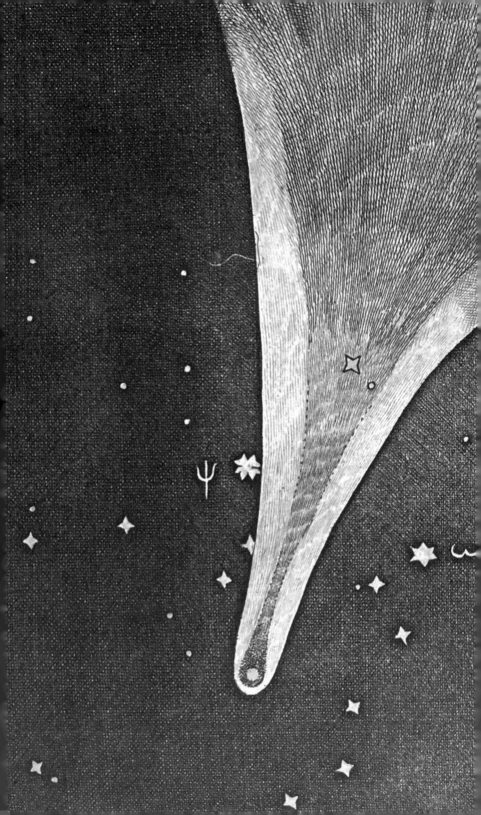